I0647936

Stories from God's Heart

God's Heart

the parables

To Diane + Clare,

Yours in Christ,

J— B——

6-14-06

guidelines
for LIVING

Stories from God's Heart

the parables

John H. Beukema

MOODY PRESS
CHICAGO

© 2000 by
JOHN HENRY BEUKEMA JR.

All Scripture quotations, unless indicated, are taken from the *Holy Bible: New International Version*®. NIV®. Copyright © 1973, 1978, 1984 by International Bible Society. Used by permission of Zondervan Publishing House. All rights reserved.

The "NIV" and "New International Version" trademarks are registered in the United States Patent and Trademark Office by International Bible Society. Use of either trademark requires permission of International Bible Society.

Library of Congress Cataloging-in-Publication Data

Beukema, John H., 1958-
    Stories from God's heart : ten parables calling us to a life worth living / John Beukema.
        p. cm.
    ISBN 0-8024-8689-4 (trade pbk.)
    1. Jesus Christ--Parables. 2. Christian life--Biblical teaching.
I. Title.

BT375.2 .B477 2000
226.8'06--dc21

                                                    00-025757

1 3 5 7 9 10 8 6 4 2

Printed in the United States of America

To Amy, always my first reader

Contents

Introduction

The messenger marched down the main street of the town. All along the way, he called out to the people in a loud and authoritative voice. He had a truth of vital importance to announce. Yet, as soon as people turned to the sound of his voice, they ran away or shouted at him to leave them alone. The townspeople wanted nothing to do with him, or his words. You see, the messenger wore no clothes as he delivered his message. He was as naked as a newborn baby. This messenger was Truth. As Truth trudged through the town speaking to no one in particular, he came upon the house of Story. "In despair he asked, 'Story, why is it that people always run away from me, but they will listen to you for hours on end?' Story smiled and said, 'It's your nakedness. If you would only wear some of my clothing, people would listen to you as never before.' So Truth agreed to put on Story's clothing and adorned himself with imagination and drama."[1]

The color and cover of story communicate truth effectively. Jesus' use of story and parable is one reason He was such a popular teacher. It was also because He taught with authority, unlike the other teachers of His day. However, through His use of parables, Jesus not only made truth memorable and easy to listen to but also obscured it. After telling the parable of the Sower and the Seed (see chapter 1 of this book), Jesus was asked to explain the meaning. Rather than answering His disciples' question immediately, He gave insight as to why He used parables at all.

> His disciples asked him what this parable meant. He said, "The knowledge of the secrets of the kingdom of God has been given to you, but to others I speak in parables, so that,
>   "'though seeing, they may not see;
>   though hearing, they may not understand.'"
>   —Luke 8:9–10

This sounds cryptic to us. It is more than a little strange to our ears. Yet, Jesus had a real purpose in making parables a primary teaching method. They were mysteries from the Master. To those, like the disciples, who were open to receive instruction from Jesus, these stories would help them to understand, and truth would be illuminated. To those who didn't truly believe, who were looking for superficial benefits and external wonders from Jesus, the stories were obscurities. They wouldn't get it. Each story Jesus told was fascinating, captivating to the crowds, but many people didn't have a clue about the meaning. As Walter Liefeld observes, "The very parable that reveals truth to some hides it from others."[2] In a sense, this was an act of grace to those who didn't believe. If they rejected explicit truth, they would receive even greater judgment. The parables veiled the truth enough so that only those who really believed would grasp their deepest meaning.

Jesus has dressed deep truths in the brilliant hues and unforgettable garment of parable. Each story is distinguished and yet disguised, obvious and yet obscure. In studying these parables, I have come to an even deeper appreciation of the wisdom and glory of Jesus. My desire to follow Him has become more passionate. My conviction of what it means to be a disciple has been sharpened. My understanding of what makes a life worth living has been challenged. I hope and pray that you will see the truths of Jesus emerging from beneath the clothes of parable. As each is revealed, may you glimpse a little more of the heart of God.

Notes

1. Harry Shields, "From His Story to Our Story: A Training Manual for Developing Narrative Sermons" (Doctor of Ministry Project, Trinity Evangelical Divinity School, Deerfield, Ill., 1996), 1.
2. Walter Liefeld, in *The Expositor's Bible Commentary,* ed. Frank E. Gaebelein, D. A. Carson, Walter W. Wessel, and Walter L. Liefeld (Grand Rapids: Zondervan, 1984), 8:906.

chapter one

For the Hearing Impaired

"The Sower and the Seed"
Luke 8:4–15

I was in the middle of a physical exam about a dozen years ago when the doctor said, "Uh oh." I didn't like the sound of that, even if he was only peering into my ears at the time. "What do you see?" I asked as casually as possible.

"I think I may have found Jimmy Hoffa," he said.

Of all the physicians in the world, I get Dr. "Shecky." It was his professional way of telling me that I had an excessive amount of earwax that needed to be removed. My comedian with a stethoscope marveled that I was able to hear at all, given the dense mass blocking my ear canal. He began digging and scraping it all away, then wanted to display what he had found. I was amazed at how much better I was able to hear when he was finished. So I asked what I could do to prevent such a problem in the future. He said there was nothing I could do other than have him clean my ears every five years or so. Since I don't voluntarily go to the doctor any more than once or twice a decade, I have tried to have my ears excavated every so often. It is an easy fix for my hearing problem.

There are other times when my hearing problem has nothing to do with excessive waxy buildup. It happened not long ago when my wife was talking to me. She was speaking on a very interesting subject, although I don't recall what it was. I was listening, but she happened to be communicating as the Chicago Cubs came to bat. The television was located over her right shoulder. Sammy Sosa stepped into the batter's box. I had one ear tuned to the Cubs' announcers and the other ear fixed upon my wife's voice, nodding at the appropriate times. With dastardly cunning she slipped in some absurd comment like, "And that was the day I became a penguin." I am certain this is against the rules of the Geneva Convention and a completely unfair tactic in marriage. I tried to explain to her, "Honey, Sammy Sosa was up. Sammy Sosa!" But I was caught. Beyond anything the doctor can pull out of my ears, I can also exhibit a selective hearing problem.

There are many different reasons why we have difficulty hearing and receiving what God says. The parables and stories Jesus used graphically grabbed the attention of those listening. Yet various hearing impairments kept the message from taking root in the lives of some, and the same impairments plague us still today. Hearing problems are what the parable known as the "Sower and the Seed" is all about. It is through this parable that we understand how we must respond to all other parables and to all the rest of God's truth.

The story Jesus told was actually not focused on the Sower (Jesus), nor the seed (God's Word). The parable emphasized the soils on which the seed fell. Through this parable Jesus was communicating a simple, critical truth. *The productiveness of our lives depends upon how we receive God's Word.* In calling people to His kingdom, Jesus made clear that how we receive the Word of God is fundamental to productive living. We can experience a deafness to God's truth that may be the result of blockage, distraction, or selective hearing.

Why did Jesus tell this parable? Luke describes what was happening at the time. "While a large crowd was gathering and people were coming to Jesus from town after town, he told this parable" (Luke 8:4). Waves of people began to lap at Jesus' heels. Crowd control was inadequate, and so many pressed in on Him that Jesus got into a boat and taught the people from a safe distance. It was this very parable that He spoke to those crowding the shoreline of the lake.

This vast gathering had many reasons for wanting to be near Him. Some intensely desired to be His followers; others were merely curious. Some longed to hear His teaching; others anxiously waited for Him to say the wrong thing so that they could indict Him. Jesus told this parable to separate the serious from the shallow, the fervent from the frivolous. This story has the power to separate still today. It identifies those who are ready to be impacted by God's Word and those who are not. Read the parable itself before considering Jesus' explanation.

> "A farmer went out to sow his seed. As he was scattering the seed, some fell along the path; it was trampled on, and the birds of the air ate it up. Some fell on rock, and when it came up, the plants withered because they had no moisture. Other seed fell among thorns, which grew up with it and choked the plants. Still other seed fell on good soil. It came up and yielded a crop, a hundred times more than was sown."
>
> When he said this, he called out, "He who has ears to hear, let him hear." (Luke 8:5–8)

This parable is notably important for two reasons. First, it is one of the few parables recorded in three of the Gospels: Matthew, Mark, and Luke. Second, it is a parable that Jesus explains. We aren't left wondering what He meant. The image Jesus used was very familiar to those listening. There by the Sea of Galilee was some of the most fertile land in Israel. Every year around November, when the rains softened the hard soil, the farmers would go out to the fields to sow their seed. It was a decidedly low-tech operation. The sower would carry his seed in the fold of his outer garment, casting it by hand. There would be pathways around him where he and others walked. There would be soil that was rocky underneath, as well as ground that hid the kernels of thorns ready to sprout with the next rainfall. But most of the seed the sower threw would find good ground, and after he had scattered it all, he would plow it under and await the harvest. Just an ordinary day for a farmer in Jesus' time, but the implications were obviously profound and the disciples wanted to make certain they didn't miss the meaning. So Jesus proceeded to explain His story.

"This is the meaning of the parable: The seed is the word of God. Those along the path are the ones who hear, and then the devil comes and takes away the word from their hearts, so that they may not believe and be saved. Those on the rock are the ones who receive the word with joy when they hear it, but they have no root. They believe for a while, but in the time of testing they fall away. The seed that fell among thorns stands for those who hear, but as they go on their way they are choked by life's worries, riches and pleasures, and they do not mature. But the seed on good soil stands for those with a noble and good heart, who hear the word, retain it, and by persevering produce a crop." (Luke 8:11–15)

Jesus was unambiguous regarding the meaning of this parable. The four types of soil illustrated the four types of hearers of God's Word. All people were represented by those four groups. Every one of us can find our place in the parable. In fact, most of us fit into all four categories at one time or another in our lives. Jesus was challenging His followers to readily and completely receive God's Word. Unless we do, a productive life will elude us. Let's take a look at the four responses to God's Word that determine how productive our lives will be.

LACK OF PREPARATION KEEPS US
FROM RECEIVING GOD'S WORD

I've never been much good at growing anything. Even the ability to produce a nice lawn has always eluded me. Year after year I planted grass seed in sparsely covered, ugly areas in my front yard. I dug into the hard earth and attempted to coax the seeds under the cover of the baked clay soil. Finally one spring I gave up and ordered a truckload of topsoil delivered. I spread a layer of loam over my pseudolawn, seeded it heavily, then raked it under. Yet no matter how hard I worked, many seeds remained on the surface. Worse still, my new soil did not adequately cover up the demon-possessed lawn underneath. The next morning my front yard looked like a scene from an Alfred Hitchcock movie. Enormous flocks of birds came from the four corners of the earth to feast at my expense. Needless to say, when my new lawn did sprout, serious bare patches remained.

It is this kind of unwelcoming, unproductive soil that Jesus uses to describe a person who is unprepared to receive God's Word. Notice that Jesus says that he hears the Word but is not prepared to *receive* it. Like seeds on a hard path, the message has no place to implant itself. There is no lasting impression, no good result, no impact at all because the Enemy won't let the seed hang around. Like hungry birds, the Evil One snatches away the Word before it can germinate. God's enemy seizes the Word from our unprepared hearts before it has any chance to bring about change. Jesus stated the very purpose of the devil in this action: "so that they may not believe and be saved" (Luke 8:12). The devil has the opposite agenda to God's. He is at cross-purposes. In reality, when we have a heart that is not prepared to receive God's Word we are cooperating with Satan himself.

How do we know if a lack of preparation is keeping us from receiving God's Word? Appearances can be misleading. A path is a very useful, busy, and necessary thing. Yet even though it is where the action is, there can be very little life. The very fact that it is a well-worn path means that there is a trampled hardness that is difficult to penetrate. Lack of preparation has many birthplaces.

- It comes from our indifference to God's truth and our lack of desire for or expectation of hearing from God.
- It comes from the busyness of our lives, from a tired familiarity with eternal truths.
- It comes from a casual apathy to the sin that sprouts defiantly within us. A heart infested with many things is not conducive to hearing from God.
- It comes from a fixation on our own agenda that depletes the force of the Word in our lives.
- It comes from an absence of willingness to exert the energy necessary to hear from God; we expect that if God really had something to say, He would take drastic measures to get our attention.

Make no mistake, the Word of God has power beyond what we can imagine. Yet Jesus tells us that the seed won't beat its way into the soil. The soil must be ready to receive it, or nothing of consequence will result. I agree with the comment Helmut Thielicke makes about such hearers: "People who are always on the go are the most in danger."[1]

It is the frenetic pace of our lives that hardens us to the Word. We rush into a Sunday morning worship service without a moment's preparation. At the benediction we stampede out again to some vastly different event: our kid's piano recital; a birthday party; the football game on TV; that new number-one movie; meal preparation; family outings. So it happens that reading Scripture, hearing a sermon, or participating in a Bible study has little impact because we are hardened by our circumstances, relationships, and packed schedules. The seed of God's Word bounces off the hardpan of our well-traveled hearts and Satan swoops in to snatch it away before the Word does any accidental "damage" in spite of our lack of readiness.

I remember an interview with Hughes Downs, host of ABC's *20/20,* where he illustrated the necessity of simply being ready to listen. Early in his career Downs was doing a radio interview with a man who had been imprisoned in Stalin's Russia and escaped. This remarkable man described how the prisoners had been digging for months, tunneling toward freedom outside the prison walls. He told of how they disposed of the dirt, including eating it. Finally late one night they were ready to break free. They sawed through a wooden barrier overhead and crawled out the hole. The man told Downs how shocked he was to find himself standing in the middle of Josef Stalin's office. I'm sure that as you read these words, dozens of questions pop into your mind. That is a thrilling account that certainly needs a conclusion. But instead of any follow-up questions, Downs asked the man, "Do you have any hobbies?" Hugh Downs had not really been listening and was not truly prepared to hear what the guest had to say. The interview, which could have been a great success, was instead a distinct failure.

Our lack of readiness to hear from God will prove to be much more costly. We must turn over the hard soil of our hearts with the spadework of expectation and fertilize the tired ground with the nutrients of desire for God. We must be willing to do the hard work of preparation, or God's truth will be snatched away before we realize that it has arrived. Jesus warns that we had better be prepared to receive God's Word or we will end up with nothing at all.

SUPERFICIAL EMOTION KEEPS US
FROM RECEIVING GOD'S WORD

I have heard the following story several times, always from someone who swears that it is true and that he or she knows the people involved. Although I can't vouch for the factual authenticity, I have no trouble believing this could have happened. The story involves a young couple who had been dating for some time. Finally the gentleman asked his vision of loveliness to marry him. She enthusiastically said yes. Their days of engagement included many more dates, as well as premarital counseling sessions. They planned and prepared for the special day that was to be their wedding, the glorious beginning to eternal bliss.

Just a few weeks before the ceremony, the intrepid groom-to-be stopped by to visit his true love unexpectedly one Saturday morning. No, he didn't find her in the arms of another. It was worse. He found her in curlers and without makeup. Horrified at this tragic sight, he bolted. Upon regaining his composure he called and broke the engagement. How superficial, how shallow— and what a blessing he discovered this fatal flaw before the wedding rather than the day after.

Is intense emotion out of place? Never. Is it a sufficient foundation upon which to build a solid relationship? Seldom. In order to stand the storms of adversity, mere emotion must develop a more substantial foundation. Such is the problem with those people who receive God's Word with joy but don't put down roots beyond that initial emotion. There must be an intellectual connection that develops with the emotional one, or the joy will be short-lived. Jesus declared that the greatest commandment is to "love the Lord your God with all your heart and with all your soul and with all your mind" (Matthew 22:37; Jesus is quoting Deuteronomy 6:5; see also Leviticus 19:18). Yes, the mind and soul are a part of loving, just as the heart is. Anything less is an insufficient foundation that will not survive the test of time.

In this parable there is no initial indication that the seed which falls on rocky ground is any different from that which falls on good soil. One cannot see the rocks lurking beneath the surface. The initial response of such a hearer is excitement, enthusiasm. Yet truth is not allowed to penetrate deeply. The initial response has no lasting effect, but remains superficial, unable to develop.

What are those obstacles that keep us from putting down roots, hindering the growth of God's Word? How can we respond so joyfully to truth at times, and then allow difficulty to wilt our excitement for God? What are those rocky places beneath the surface of our lives, and how do they get there?

- They come from disappointment when God fails to meet our expectations. We count on God to do this or change that—and nothing happens. Disenchantment overtakes us, drying up the moisture needed for proper root growth.
- They come from an unwillingness to put any work into our spiritual relationship. God's Word is demanding, but we can't be bothered with long-time exercise. So no biblical foundation is built, no scriptural muscles are developed, and temptation topples the structure.
- They come from a stubbornness that refuses to give up certain attractions that stunt the growth of God's Word within us.
- They come from an attachment to a teacher, a tradition, a structure, a schedule, an achievement, an attitude, a comfort, a cause, a position, a power, a bias, or a bitterness that is deeper than our attachment to the things of God.

Several years ago, the church I pastored was part of a citywide evangelistic effort. After it concluded, we received the names of dozens of people for follow up. These individuals had signed commitment cards indicating a newfound faith in Christ. I was amazed and saddened by how quickly the joyful response had faded from the majority of those we contacted. A high school senior had already buckled under to the mere possibility of ridicule from his classmates and was not willing to risk being ostracized from his peer group. A thirty-something man at first talked about all the changes that God was bringing about in his life, yet he was not ready to attend a Bible-believing church. He felt he should return to the church of his childhood, even while admitting that his childhood church was merely a cultural institution, one that offered no opportunity for spiritual growth. His reasoning was based on not wanting to offend his family. Within a brief period of time this man had completely fallen away from the Word he had once joyfully received. Finally there was the single mother who had returned home to bills that were still unpaid, children that were still out of control, and relationships that were still disintegrating. Her emotional response to the gospel had brought great joy and hope initially. But it had put down no roots and soon withered under the arid test of daily life. We must banish those rocks lurking an inch below the surface, or the life-giving Word will not grow for long. Jesus tells us that mere enthusiasm, a superficial emotional acceptance of God's Word, will never endure the temptations and trials that will certainly come our way.

LIFE'S DISTRACTIONS KEEP US
FROM RECEIVING GOD'S WORD

The Brooklyn Bridge is one of the marvels of human creation in North America. The builders accomplished this monumental undertaking more than one hundred years ago, despite countless obstacles and accidents. The cable-wire suspension bridge was the first of its kind in the world. When the bridge was finally opened to the public, it was a huge curiosity. Pedestrians traveled between Manhattan and Brooklyn for a small fee. Tragically it was during one of those times that the bridge was packed with people that someone shouted, "The bridge is falling!" This thoughtless joke created a panic in the crowd and twelve people were trampled to death in the stampede to get off the bridge.

How similar to the fate of the seed that fell among

the thorns. Jesus equates the thorns with the pleasures of this world that choke out our receptivity to the Word. The heavy traffic of other thoughts, desires, business, activities, and enjoyable pursuits tramples the seed into oblivion. The panicky rush of many other things squashes the life from God's truth within us.

This type of hearer that Jesus identifies does receive the truth and goes on his or her way. But a problem develops stemming from a preoccupation with the stuff of life. Those pleasures of life are any peripheral pursuits and extraneous experiences that are allowed to overwhelm the life-giving Word. They erode and corrode the impact of God's Word little by little.

These distractions in and of themselves are not sinful or wrong, yet they smother the Word so that it produces nothing. As Douglas Beyer explains, "A weed is nothing but a plant out of place."[2] The thorns and weeds that strangle the productivity of the Word may well be wholesome, family oriented, and responsible. Yet because they are out of place, they have a negative impact on the Word. The seed doesn't ripen, mature, or yield anything. The truth of God is not suddenly snatched away or assaulted by some force in this instance. Instead, it dies out gradually, crowded out by the quest for and the enjoyment of other things. William Hendriksen describes the disastrous implications of these distractions. "Like a proliferating cancer gradually killing the body, or a destructive parasite little by little destroying its host, so also these 'thorns' slowly but surely choke the souls of those people who extend a welcome to them. Such individuals never mature."[3]

One difference between this hearer and the first two is that this person doesn't fall away. But once the Word is suffocated by the weeds, there is simply no growth.

The mixture of thorns and seeds is an attempt to unite two incompatible elements. Thorns do not play well with others. They take over. They are to the garden what Latrell Sprewell is to basketball. Latrell Sprewell is the young professional basketball player who took exception to how P. J. Carlissimo was coaching him. Angered, he attacked Carlissimo right during practice. After being stopped once, Sprewell returned and abused the coach again. Sprewell reportedly had his hands clamped around his coach's throat, attempting to choke him, until he was pulled away by fellow players. That image is very appropriate to describe the word Jesus uses in relation to the thorns. Jesus says that they strangle, throttle the seed.

What are the thorns we allow into our lives? When do we become so preoccupied, when do our lives become so cluttered that these distractions choke the life from God's Word?

- When God's truth becomes only one of many loyalties, interests, and passions.
- When we are intellectually promiscuous, accepting all kinds of seeds without differentiation. These cultural obsessions, popular opinions, and standards of living seem just as valid and important as God's Word.
- When we give so much attention to our entertainment, hobbies, career advancement, investments, or health that the impact of the Word is diluted.
- When following after Christ is squeezed into the crevices of our lives, scribbled into the margins rather than being the focal point of who we are.
- When any single event, experience, or pursuit can take us away from worship.

I often encounter professing Christians who have made these kinds of choices. They are the soccer moms and dads who believe that taking Junior to his Sunday morning soccer game takes precedence over worship and biblical instruction. They are the business people who consistently choose to go into the office instead of to church, claiming that it is something that they "have" to do. They are the sports fans who have season tickets and simply must go to the game, or the golfers who have Sunday morning tee-off times that just can't be given up. They are the family cooks who are so consumed with offering great meals for family gatherings that they have no time to offer God anything in worship or to enjoy a spiritual meal for themselves. These are the simple things that retard the productivity of God's Word in us. The stunting of spiritual development is seldom a one-time decision, but rather a series of seemingly innocuous choices that eventually overwhelm the life force of God's Word.

Jazz musician Kurt Whalum found thorns choking the productivity of God's Word in his life. In an interview with *New Man* magazine in the summer of 1995, Whalum described the changes in his life. Despite a desire to seek after God and a hunger for the Word in his younger days, Whalum's passion for music began to claim his greater interest. He had left his first love. But then God broke through the distractions.

It happened as I prepared for speech class at Texas Southern University. I thought I would use something from the Bible to make my speech sound profound. I took my Bible off the shelf and it was covered with dust. When I opened it, a dead bug fell out! That moment my thought was certainly from the Holy Spirit: *That dead bug is just like you are without Me in your life.* Those words hit me hard! God

wasn't at all telling me to quit music. He just knew I needed Him to call the shots in my life. So I devoted myself to
study of the Scripture and prayer.[4]

It was after this commitment that Kirk's career took
off. He recorded and sold thousands of albums and per-
formed with the biggest names in the music industry.
Soon this popularity, success, and constant travel confronted Kirk with another decision. Rather than spend
more time away from his family and his men's group
Bible study, he gave up touring.

There is nothing wrong with a passion for music, the
pleasure it gives, and the success it can bring. It is no
different from the many different pleasures and passions
that can capture our attention. The problem comes when
these "plants" are out of place. Jesus tells us that such
affections out of control will insidiously strangle the
productivity of God's Word in our lives.

BEAUTIFUL TENACITY MAKES
GOD'S WORD PRODUCTIVE IN US

Ray Stedman tells the story of Dr. Kern, a German
college professor. Dr. Kern was a member of the Luther-
an Church, which was the state church. Stedman relates
a marvelous occurrence in this man's life.

> He attended only a couple of times a year, he had nev-
> er read the Bible, and he had no knowledge of the things
> of Christ. But because Dr. Kern was a prominent citizen,
> the church asked him to serve on the board. He agreed
> and worked diligently. His efforts then resulted in his be-
> ing asked to serve at the state level, and ultimately on the
> governing council of the church for the entire nation.
> When the professor reached that level, he became
> convinced that he ought to know something, at least, of

the Christian faith. So he took two weeks' vacation and went alone to a quiet retreat where he began to read the Bible. He became so fascinated that he read on and on, sometimes even missing meals, until at the end of the first week he knelt down in his room and cried out to the Lord to save him. The next week he deliberately missed his meals, fasting through the week, and continued to read until he had completed the entire Bible. Dr. Kern returned to his position of leadership a new man and became a catalyst for change in the government of the church. He is now a powerful voice, calling people to reintroduce God and the Scriptures into the dead machinery of the church. That is what the Word of God can do.[5]

The story of Dr. Kern serves as a fine example of the productivity of the Word in good soil. I use the phrase "beautiful tenacity" to picture what Jesus says about this kind of person. Jesus has thoroughly described what keeps us from receiving God's Word, but He doesn't leave us there. Jesus would not have bothered to tell the parable if it were not possible for the defective hearers to become effective. Alexander MacLaren confidently states, "These different types of character are capable of being changed."[6] So the final words of Jesus are crucial. Here is how we can live productively. Here is how the Word can explode with growth in our lives. Note the specific words Jesus uses to explain the productive soil. "But the seed on good soil stands for those with a noble and good heart, who hear the word, retain it, and by persevering produce a crop" (Luke 8:15).

Just who is ready to hear God? Those who have a pure character, who won't let go, and who are willing to wait. Jesus uses this threefold description to show us the type of person who is receptive to God's Word. Let's look at each one of them.

Those Who Have Pure Character

Jesus first refers to a "noble and good heart." The word translated *noble* means to be free from defects. It was used of a flawless pearl. The same word was used by the disciples when they saw the "beautiful" stones adorning the temple (Luke 21:5). Jesus also uses the word *good* to describe those whose hearts are receptive to the Word. This goodness refers to a moral purity; to what is right and beneficial. Jesus says that this beauty —this purity of character—is a prerequisite for receiving His Word.

That certainly speaks to those whose lack of preparation keeps the Word from being productive. As William Hendriksen notes, "The character of the hearer determines the effect of the Word upon him."[7] If our character is impure, morally corrupt, and defective, then the ground of our hearts is not prepared to receive the seed of the Word of God. For those who have been made children of God through faith in Christ, a lack of purity can block the power of God's Word. True believers have very simple instructions for handling this situation. The epistle of James makes it clear: "Get rid of all moral filth and the evil that is so prevalent and humbly accept the word planted in you, which can save you" (James 1:21).

This is a call to God's people to clean up. The phrase "get rid of" is used in connection with changing clothes. Strip off like dirty clothes the sin that contaminates you. Without such cleansing our sin will smear the viewing window to truth. William Gurnall once warned, "The Holy God will not take a filthy hand and lead you into understanding." When we come clean before God, confessing our sin, He faithfully forgives. It is that purity of character that opens us up to hearing from God. It is that clean beauty that allows His Word to be productive in our lives.

Those Who Won't Let Go

Jesus next mentions those who "retain" the Word. Rather than letting the Word be snatched away or wither from lack of moisture, these hearers hold fast, guard, and take possession of the truth. The same expression is used in Luke 4:42. Jesus had done great miracles, healing all the sick and demon possessed that were brought to Him. He worked until the darkness fell. Early the next morning He got up to find a place to be alone. Undoubtedly, He was going to speak to the Father and renew energies drained by the vast needs of the crowds. But the people found Him and held on, trying their best to keep Him from going away ("stayed him," KJV).

That is the understanding of the Word *retain* Jesus uses here. I was twenty years old when I began preaching. I remember those earliest attempts to communicate God's truth. Each opportunity seemed to fill me with exhilaration or crushing discouragement. There was a lovely, saintly, elderly woman in that congregation who made me her special encouragement project. Sometime after that initial sermon I received my first note from Mary Pack. In her spidery handwriting, that dear woman filled me with hope that God could use even me. I treasured that note, and each of the next dozen I received. Each envelope that arrived was ripped open with joy and anticipation. Even those times when I felt an utter failure, God used those little pages to lift me up. I still have them.

Even though Mrs. Pack went to be with the Lord long ago, her notes still encourage me twenty years later.

Going beyond *hearing* the Word to *retaining* the Word involves seeing the Word the way I saw those notes. Longing to hear from God. Basking in His encouragement, love, and instruction. Treasuring the communication of truth. Not wanting to let go of what He has revealed.

Those Who Are Willing to Wait

In the final part of His explanation, Jesus includes the need to produce a good crop "by persevering." The good hearers hang in there at all costs until harvest time. They don't give up until the results arrive. This is the patient endurance like that required for the century plant. Actually the plant is misnamed. It was erroneously thought only to bloom every one hundred years. The truth is you don't have to wait that long—it just seems like it. This desert plant produces no flowers and evidences no growth for two or three decades. It exists in arid conditions at about the height of a man for all those years. Then suddenly this barren, spiky-looking plant will explode with growth. At the rate of half a foot per day, the plant will reach heights of forty feet. Then the century plant goes into bloom for several weeks, displaying yellow flowers. It's a long wait, but heaven forbid that you give up after ten years and cut it down.

So it is with those who are receptive to the Word. If you persevere, eventually—if you are willing to wait—there will be a great harvest. Jesus uses this same word for perseverance in Luke 21:19 ("standing firm"). Here He tells His disciples that they have persecution in their future. They will face hatred and the threat of death. He calls them to "stand firm," hang in there, and see it through. This kind of stamina is the type that bears much fruit. It is in the lives of these hearers that the harvest is a hundred times what was sown. At the very least this would be an extraordinary harvest. Neither wheat nor barley produce that much normally. Jesus is saying that the power of the seed in the right soil will produce beyond our expectations and imaginations.

It is a beautiful tenacity that allows God's Word to be productive in us. A beauty that comes from a pure, moral character, with no defects to stunt the growth of the Word. A tenacity that refuses to let the seed of truth drift out of our lives but hangs on, patiently waiting for the blossoms to come.

The power of this well-known parable should jolt us out of our comfortable, cruise-control existence. In order to live productively, to have God's Word blossom in us, we should long to be the kind of hearer Jesus describes. This does not require sophistication or great education. It simply requires a beautiful tenacity in response to the hearing of the Word. This is what author Bob George found in Wilber, a luxury limousine driver. Bob was delighted to find that Wilber was a brother in Christ. They had fellowship together all the way to the airport. Somewhere along the way Bob was astonished to discover that Wilber didn't own a Bible. He was anxious to change that and asked permission to mail Wilber a Bible right away. It was then that Wilber admitted to a further complication—he didn't know how to read. Bob writes of his amazement.

> Here was a man with as solid a grasp on biblical truth as I had ever encountered, and yet he was saying that he didn't even have the ability to read the Bible. "Then how have you learned so much, Wilber?" I asked. His big grin returned. "I may not be able to read, Mr. George, but I listen real good! I love Jesus, and so whenever I get a chance to learn some more about Him in church or on the radio, I

perk up my ears and pray that God will teach me. And He always does."[8]

I would classify Wilber as a noble and good heart, one who hears the Word, retains it, and perseveres to produce a good crop. It is that type of person Jesus says will live productively. The critical point is how we receive the truth God broadcasts for us. The productiveness of our lives depends upon how we receive God's Word. Faced with that understanding, we need to confront Jesus' parable personally. Where am I right now in terms of my receptivity to God's Word? Don't let a hearing impairment keep you from living productively.

Notes

1. Helmut Thielicke, *The Waiting Father,* trans. John Doberstein (New York: Harper & Row, 1959), 54.
2. Douglas Beyer, *Parables for Christian Living* (Valley Forge, Pa.: Judson, 1985), 20.
3. William Hendriksen, *Exposition of the Gospel According to Luke,* New Testament Commentary (Grand Rapids: Baker, 1978), 428.
4. Dave Geisler, "Cover Story," *New Man* (July/August 1995), 22–24.
5. Ray C. Stedman, *Waiting for the Second Coming* (Grand Rapids: Discovery House, 1990), 142–43.
6. Alexander MacLaren, *Expositions of Holy Scripture,* vol. 9, *St. Luke* (reprint, Grand Rapids: Baker, 1984), 235.
7. Hendriksen, *Exposition of the Gospel According to Luke,* 426.
8. Bob George, *Growing in Grace* (Eugene, Oreg.: Harvest House, 1991), 54–55.

chapter two

Love at Street Level

"The Good Samaritan"
Luke 10:25–37

It was the night before Thanksgiving. Twenty of us were part of a team helping to prepare and serve Thanksgiving dinner for homeless people in Chicago. Our church supplied the pie, and we had received far more than needed. When the meal was over, hundreds of little plates with pieces of apple and pumpkin pie littered the serving tables. We pondered how to store the leftovers. Suddenly someone suggested that we deliver the pie to other homeless people on our way home. We loaded up, all the while discussing where would be the best places to go. The first stop was the Pacific Garden Mission. When we arrived, we could see a service going on at that very moment. It was packed with people. Those in charge welcomed the dozens and dozens of slices of pie we unloaded. With the remainder we decided to drive down Lower Wacker Drive. This underground street is a well-known location for homeless people in Chicago. It wasn't long before we spotted an enclave of the homeless, their belongings and collectibles piled around them. As we pulled to a stop, I was amazed to see my (not quite fourteen-year-old) daughter burst from the van. She charged toward the cluster of people brandishing plates of pie. Afterward I told her that she shouldn't have run on ahead; it wasn't safe.

"I think that's what I want to do with my life," she said.

I chuckled. "What? Deliver slabs of pie to street people?"

"I don't mean just pie, Dad. I mean helping people like this."

I was proud of my daughter. Our family has so much; I was glad to see that she realized how little some others have and was moved to act. She could have been afraid, embarrassed, or worse, looked down on those men. Instead she eagerly involved herself in this little act of kindness.

I am sorry to say that I don't always have that reaction when confronted with people in need. Yet that is the point Jesus makes very clearly in the parable of the Good Samaritan. Notice what prompted Jesus to tell this story.

> On one occasion an expert in the law stood up to test Jesus. "Teacher," he asked, "what must I do to inherit eternal life?"
>
> "What is written in the Law?" he replied. "How do you read it?"
>
> He answered: "'Love the Lord your God with all your heart and with all your soul and with all your strength and with all your mind'; and, 'Love your neighbor as yourself.'"
>
> "You have answered correctly," Jesus replied. "Do this and you will live."
>
> But he wanted to justify himself, so he asked Jesus, "And who is my neighbor?" (Luke 10:25–29)

The first question the lawyer asks was one that many people were wondering about then and wonder about now. He was not alone in his desire to discover how to attain eternal life. William Hendriksen defines it this way: "It refers to the kind of life that is not only endless in duration but also priceless in quality."[1] Who wouldn't want such an existence? Yet it seems that this expert in the Law was not completely sincere in asking this question. His motives may not have been entirely pure. He was testing Jesus in some way, perhaps examining His grasp of the books of Moses. After all, that was the area of specialty for this legal eagle. He may have wanted to demonstrate his superior knowledge and embarrass Jesus. This was not much different from what happened years ago at a pastor's conference I attended. The speaker was a well-known author. Early in his presentation a man in the audience stood and said, "I have a question." The man then asked a question that he himself answered in depth for fifteen minutes. Before he was through enlightening us, this guru in sheep's clothing had marched to the front, drawn diagrams on the board, and left us shaking our heads in amused annoyance. Once he had displayed his intellectual superiority over this professional we had all paid to hear, the budding prodigy sat down. Such a mixed motive may have been present in this lawyer's inquiry.

Jesus countered the question with a question. He invited the man to display his knowledge of the Law and to give his personal interpretation. Jesus showed that whatever answer he gave to the question of eternal life would not be something new, but rather something already revealed by God.

The lawyer was up to the task. He summarized the requirements of the law, restating Deuteronomy 6:5 and

Leviticus 19:18. Perfect love toward God and neighbor brings the promise of eternal life. Jesus authenticated his answer. When He called it correct, Jesus used the Greek word *orthos,* from which we get words like *orthopedic* and *orthodox*. The answer was straight, proper, and right. Assuring him that he knew the proper path, Jesus said in effect, "Just do it."

Before we go further, it is important to note the reality of this statement. Such a task is impossible. No one can love God so completely and neighbors so intimately all the time. The truth is we are unable to keep the commandments that qualify us for eternal life. That is precisely the point. It was exactly for this reason that Jesus came. We cannot fulfill the demands of the Law.

The Law spotlights the fact that we fall short of God's standard. As a youngster I spent time at several different farms of various church families. Many of those experiences were during haying season. My main duty on the hay wagon seemed to involve staying out of everyone else's way. "Don't get too near the bailer; you'll fall in and get trussed up like a Butterball turkey." "Don't stand in the way of the chute. The bale will knock you off and the wagon wheels will squash you like a grape." Evidently all the exciting stuff would result in my untimely death.

But I wanted to show that I was a farmer just like Kurt, Larry, Irv, and Grandpa Moore. These guys got to grab the new bale off the chute, carry it to the back of the wagon, and hoist it up on top of the other bales. I begged and pleaded for my chance. Finally they gave in. Looking back decades later, I can imagine that they were all grinning as I positioned my adolescent body at the end of the baling chute. I was planning to catch that bale and stack it like a pro. What a surprise when the bale came and I folded under it like cheap lawn furniture.

In effect, that is what God does with the Law. We cannot possibly do all that God demands; therefore, we are all guilty, sinful people. In our attempts to inherit eternal life, we end up underneath, crushed by the weight of our own sin, trapped by the weakness of our own righteousness. The Law shows us how inadequate and unable we are to meet God's standard. But Jesus met the requirements of the Law with a perfect life. Then He paid the penalty for the sin of others by His suffering and death. Following that sacrificial death, He declared the victory by His resurrection. Through Christ, all those who believe are forgiven, made righteous and acceptable to a holy God. He bore the crushing weight of my sin so that I wouldn't have to.

The lawyer knew the answer, but he also knew that he couldn't keep it. Instead of trapping or embarrassing Jesus, he himself felt trapped and uncertain. Cornered, he looked for an escape route. He needed an excuse or at least a watering down of this demanding Law. He thought, *Perhaps I can keep this requirement if I just narrow the playing field.* So he asked Jesus, "Who is my neighbor?" Many at that time assumed that the command he had just quoted to Jesus at most only related to other Israelites. The attitude was, "If you aren't an Israelite, don't expect anything from me." It would be natural, culturally expected, a communal responsibility to treat a fellow Israelite in a loving fashion. Beyond those parameters, such behavior was unthinkably difficult. To suppress his guilt and lower the bar so that he could clear it, the lawyer asked for a definition of *neighbor.* Just who is and who isn't covered by this word? Rather than giving a direct answer, Jesus told a story.

In reply Jesus said: "A man was going down from Jerusalem to Jericho, when he fell into the hands of robbers. They stripped him of his clothes, beat him and went away, leaving him half-dead. A priest happened to be going down the same road, and when he saw the man, he passed by on the other side. So too, a Levite, when he came to the place and saw him, passed by on the other side. But a Samaritan, as he traveled, came where the man was; and when he saw him, he took pity on him. He went to him and bandaged his wounds, pouring on oil and wine. The he put the man on his own donkey, took him to an inn and took care of him. The next day he took out two silver coins and gave them to the innkeeper. 'Look after him,' he said, 'and when I return, I will reimburse you for any extra expense you may have.'" (Luke 10:30–35)

The main point of the story can be described in this sentence: *If God's love is in us, it will be shown in how we treat the needy ones God puts in our path.* Although no audience is specifically mentioned beyond the lawyer, there is an implication that other people were present. Wherever Jesus went there was quite a following, even beyond His own disciples. The fact that the lawyer "stood up" signals that he made himself known from among a number of others. Perhaps Jesus was speaking at the time. The fact that the lawyer attempted to "test" Jesus suggests a desire to embarrass or prove himself superior to Jesus in front of witnesses. So it would not be a complete fabrication to imagine a wider audience than just one man.

This parable communicates powerfully today, with a clear and obvious lesson. Yet I expect there was even more punch and surprise as Jesus unfolded the story than we initially experience in reading it today. The plot twist is not in the fact that such an event could occur. Norval Geldenhuys has noted the danger of the location

Jesus identified. "The rocky, tortuous road from Jerusalem to Jericho has through all the centuries been no-
torious as a place where robbers all too often attack
travelers."[2] A violent, criminal act on that trip would
have been no surprise. Nor would it have been a shock
to most of those listening that neither the priest nor the
Levite stopped to help. They were religious, but that did-
n't translate into bravery, putting oneself out, or risking
contamination.

Such heartlessness, cowardice, or cautious nonin-
volvement was to be expected of these people. Walter
Liefeld says, "The religious leaders act contrary to love,
though not contrary to expectation."[3] The fact that the
clergy came across negatively was undoubtedly well received by anyone listening. Playful nudges, sarcastic
grins, and sly winks were probably shared among the
people as the story progressed.

No, none of those plot lines was out of the ordinary
for those in the audience. The surprising part of the tale
was who the hero turned out to be. It was not average
Joseph Israelite. It was not a layman, someone most like
those listening eagerly to the story. Rather, it was of all
things a Samaritan. Harry Ironside notes that "this was
almost the last man in the world from whom the poor,
wounded Jew had any right to expect mercy."[4]

The power and surprise of this parable announces
not only who our neighbor is but also how to be a neighbor. The story begins with a certain man. Jesus doesn't
say, but it is assumed the man is a Jew. The traveler is
going down from Jerusalem. Now in a Jewish context
there is only one direction away from Jerusalem, down.
Because of the exalted and holy status of the city, one always goes up to Jerusalem. But the trip from Jerusalem
to Jericho is down in another sense of the word. Although

they are only about seventeen miles apart, the descent is fairly steep. Jerusalem stands at 2,550 feet above sea level, while Jericho is approximately 800 feet below sea level. In this rugged terrain, escape is not really an option. The thugs surround the traveler, strip off his clothes, thrash him within an inch of his life, and leave him battered and bleeding on the road. Will anyone help him?

The story illustrates six actions we must take for the needy ones God puts in our path. Here is what we will do if we are filled with God's love.

1. WE WILL RISK INCONVENIENCE

Howard is one of the deacons in our church. He is a busy man who juggles countless work-related and ministry activities, all while exuding a vibrant testimony for Jesus Christ. One of the people assigned to Howard for pastoral care is "Walter." This young man is a challenge. "Walter" has a plethora of medical problems. His list of prescriptions is as long as your arm. He has been in and out of hospitals on a weekly basis. His medical condition, poverty, and absence of relatives have produced car accidents, court appearances, psychiatric treatments, and frequent moves. Howard has borne the brunt of all this turmoil. Late night and early morning phone calls, a crisis of the month, and frequent frustrations are the kinds of challenges that have fallen to Howard. I doubt that anyone could handle more than one "Walter" in life. As exhausting as this is, Howard hangs in there. He doesn't do it alone, but often he is the one most inconvenienced by the many needs "Walter" has. I applaud Howard and his ministry of inconvenience. It was this type of ministry with which the priest didn't want to be bothered.

In the story in Luke the priest is the first to come by. He is undoubtedly returning from duties at the temple, where he has offered sacrifices to God. When he sees the man lying in the road, he crosses over to the other side. Does this priest have no compassion? How is it possible that he would not stop to help one in such obvious need? The priest could have believed the traveler was dead. It would complicate his life to touch a dead body. Numbers 19:11 made it clear that such an action would make him unclean for seven days. Gary Inrig made a good observation. "The priest had already been away from home for a period of time, and the ritual of cleansing was costly and time consuming. At the very least, involvement would require a return to Jerusalem and the interruption of his plans."[5]

For the priest to happen upon this unfortunate man was a serious inconvenience. He moved to the other side of the road to avoid any possible contact with the victim and kept going down toward home. The whole situation might have even provoked him to praise God. "Thank you, Lord, that that wasn't me. I praise You for protecting me on my journey." Whatever the reasons, Jesus made clear that this man was not acting as he should toward the one placed in his path. He refused to risk being inconvenienced. One of the significant things that the parable of the Good Samaritan shows us is that when the love of God is in us, we will take risks.

- We will risk the inconvenience of contamination. The contamination I may face from practicing this love will not be ceremonial. It will have more to do with polluted sensibilities, decency, and judgment. I will be willing to risk the sights, sounds, smells, and sensations demanded by expressing God's love to another.

- We will risk the inconvenience of being out of our comfort zone. This kind of love may call me out from the known to the unknown. It may require me to do something I have never done before, for someone I've never dealt with before.
- We will risk the inconvenience of an interrupted schedule. This type of love may demand that my agenda change, that my plans take a backseat for the time being.

There is risk involved in showing the love of God to those He puts in our path. It was a risk that the priest was not willing to take. But Jesus made clear that one who is filled with the love of God will risk inconvenience for his or her neighbor.

2. WE WILL SACRIFICE OUR SAFETY

Bob and Marla Boulter did not plan on risking their lives or sacrificing their safety. It happened because they were doing what they believed God called them to do. This couple was involved in inner-city ministry in Washington, D.C. Bob was with Jubilee Housing, Inc. This ministry buys dilapidated buildings and turns them into cooperatively managed housing. Jubilee gives people a place to live and creates safe communities. Bob tells of a time when Marla was attacked and robbed. Afterward, they considered moving because of the danger, fear, and possible cost of ministry in that location. Following much reflection, prayer, and Scripture searching, they felt their call reaffirmed.

Just a few months later, that call was put to the test again. Bob tried to stop two men from robbing a van in the ministry parking lot. Suddenly, he was surrounded by five or six men, who attacked him. First, they beat him and pulled his wallet from his pocket. Then as Bob tried to get away, the men ran him down and tore his watch from his wrist, kicking and stomping him. Blood poured from injuries to his head. A bystander got the men to stop before they killed him. In addition to the lumps, abrasions, and cuts, Bob underwent surgery to repair broken cheekbones and broken bones in his ears. As a result, Bob has wire in his face and plastic in his ear. In intense pain, Bob also began to reflect and to consider the bigger picture.

> In short order Marla clearly perceived her mugging as a sort of preparation for her to endure and help me through my suffering, which she did in an awesome way. We were brought closer to one another in the midst of pain and difficulty. Strangely, the response of many others, even cautious family members, was to affirm, in ways not previously expressed, their support for us and our costly ministry in the inner-city. Our experience gave them an opportunity to speak of our work to others, and I think they surprised themselves with the conviction with which they answered challenges about our belonging where we were: "Why such a risk?" and "What reward could possibly make such work worthwhile?"[6]

The Levite was the next to arrive on the scene. It is interesting that both he and the priest would be traveling alone. Since the road was dangerous, it was customary to make the trip with a group of people. The journey between Jericho and Jerusalem was a popular one, for there were quite a number of men involved in temple service who lived in Jericho. The duty of a Levite was to be a helper to the priests. They assisted in the maintenance of the temple. Undoubtedly this man also had come from a time of spiritual activity.

Perhaps this Levite had the same thoughts that the priest had. He certainly had the same reaction, for he moved to the other side of the road when he spotted the robbery victim. One or both of these men probably had concern for their personal safety in mind. It was possible that what appeared to be a man in need of help was only a decoy. It had all of the potential of being a ruse. The Levite wouldn't have to be terribly imaginative to think that if he ventured close to the apparent casualty, the roadside gang might be waiting to pounce on him. He would not be trapped by such methods, so he steered clear of the potential danger. "The Levite was a man whose motto was, 'Safety first.' He would take no risks to help anyone else."[7] If he was filled with thoughts and concerns for his personal safety, it kept him from demonstrating any real love for God in this situation.

That is a fear we must confront if we claim to love God and seek to love our neighbor. Safety is an issue even when you don't live in a bad neighborhood. There is danger whenever you reach out to another. The dangers of being taken advantage of, being played for a fool, and getting hurt are all very real. This parable tells me that a willingness to sacrifice my safety is part of what it means to act out the love of God. Like Bob and Marla Boulter, I must be ready to sacrifice even my safety in order to serve how and where God calls me.

- Love is not consumed with "safety first." While I will not live recklessly, I will constantly depend upon God to protect me. I will not decide whom I will love and how I will love based upon my personal security.
- Love involves jeopardy. I understand that there is danger involved in reaching out to those God places

in my path. The risk of being used, the danger of loss, the hazard of long-term involvement are all possibilities.

• Love refuses to avoid people in need. I will not turn away from needs that lie in a heap on the path in front of me.

To whatever extent the Levite and the priest were concerned with their safety, they faced a much more serious spiritual danger in their attempt to stay safe. To know the love of God means I will be willing to sacrifice my safety to express that love to those He puts in my path.

3. WE WILL IGNORE SOCIAL BARRIERS

Jean (John) Thomas is a Haitian who carries out a ministry of community development in his native land. Jean once told me of an incident that occurred on a Sunday night in the southern United States. There was a program at the local Baptist church that he wanted to see. Jean arrived with several of his friends. The friends were all admitted, but he was not. It was simply because they were white and he was black. When Jean told me that story, what amazed me most was that it happened in 1978. Long after the heyday of the civil rights movement, Jean was refused entrance into an evangelical church. We have our share of social barriers today. Race is one of them. The racial and religious division between Samaritan and Jew was similar. Jesus made this an obvious point in the story.

There was a great barrier between the Jews and Samaritans. Most of us don't have a frame of reference to help us understand how utterly odd it would be for a Jew and Samaritan to interact in the way Jesus describes. The Jews used the word *Samaritan* as a term of contempt. The bitterness reached a crescendo less than thirty years before Jesus told this story. The historian Josephus recorded that one night during the feast of Passover, some Samaritans crept into the city of Jerusalem. Entering the temple, whose gates were opened at midnight, the intruders left male cadavers in the holy place.[8]

Whether these dead bodies were whole, in pieces, or simply skeletal remains made little difference. This was a gross pollution of the sacred, which was horrific enough by itself. But it was also done on one of the most important dates on the Jewish religious calendar, Passover. This violation caused the Jews to expel all Samaritans from temple worship. The animosity between the two groups continued long after that incident. Everyone knew it. If you wanted to curse out a Jew, simply call him a Samaritan. That was why Jesus' discussion with the woman at the well in John 4 was so unconventional. When He asked her for a drink, she couldn't believe it. Jews didn't associate with Samaritans.

With that kind of background one can imagine the thoughts when a Samaritan is the next to make an appearance in Jesus' story. If a priest and a Levite avoided the victim, this Samaritan would be expected to finish him off. What a golden opportunity to spit at, kick, or knife a member of the opposition. Yet rather than doing any of those things, or even avoiding the man lying in a heap, the Samaritan comes to his side. He is immediately compassionate for this unfortunate person. The Samaritan obviously did not look at the man and see a Jew or years of animosity; he only saw someone who needed help.

We must relate that cultural obstacle to some that

we face. This parable communicates that a willingness to ignore social barriers is part of what it means to act out the love of God.

- Love ignores the barrier of skin color. If the love of God is in me, I will seek to be free from the chains of racial bias.
- Love ignores the smell of an unwashed body. If I am filled with God's love, my preference for hygiene, my sense of smell, and my weak stomach will not keep me from exhibiting the love of God.
- Love ignores accepted differences. If God's love is a reality in me, I will not follow conventional wisdom as it relates to another person. I will let love cover a multitude of sins and impediments and will reach out in love.
- Love ignores the barrier of religious distinctions. If the love of God is in me, I will not restrict my love to those who pass my test of orthodoxy. I will express that love to heretic, pagan, and rebel alike.

Jesus pressed home the point that the person who truly loves God will climb over all social barriers to provide help to the needy one in his or her path.

4. WE WILL MOVE FROM EMOTION TO ACTION

I vividly remember a catastrophe that occurred in December of 1981. The event made a lasting impact on me even though it didn't happen to anyone I know. A plane, its wings covered with ice, crashed into a bridge and fell into the Potomac River. Passengers, both dead and alive, were spilled into the icy waters. A crowd gathered on the snowy banks as the rescue operation swung into action. The only way to reach many of those in the water was by helicopter. The helicopter was lowering a life preserver to the floating victims. But one young woman was unable to grasp the preserver. The cold water was taking its toll, and it looked as if she would surely drown. All those watching the horrifying event were concerned, but one man went beyond feelings. This bystander pushed through the crowd and the police barricade and jumped into the icy water and pulled the woman to safety.

The reason this incident stays in my memory is because of how this one man acted on his feelings of compassion and got involved. Standing on the banks of the Potomac and feeling sorry for the drowning woman would accomplish nothing. It was the willingness of one man to do something that saved her life. To move from emotion to action is what it means to demonstrate the love of God.

Of the three travelers who come upon the wounded man by the side of the road in the parable in Luke, only one is said to have felt anything for him. Obviously, the others did feel something, even if none of those feelings was pity for a man in need. Whatever it was that the priest and Levite felt, it propelled them away from the man. In great contrast, the Samaritan felt pity and was compelled to go to the man. Jesus described exactly what action the Samaritan took on behalf of the injured stranger. The actions included first aid treatment. He soothed the wounds with a salve (the oil) and disinfected them with wine. He bandaged the lacerations, and since the robbers had stripped their victim, the Samaritan probably had to use his own clothes to make bandages.

- Love must do something. Love isn't simply something I feel; it is something I do.

• Love feels the need to be involved. If the love of God is in me, I will go beyond feeling sympathy or pity for the one in need. I will feel to the point of involvement.

The parable vividly shows that one filled with the love of God cannot remain a bystander when confronted with real need.

5. WE WILL GIVE PERSONAL AND PRACTICAL ASSISTANCE

Lloyd Ogilvie tells the story of how he was given an opportunity to act out what he believed.

One Sunday noon, after preaching on the spontaneous love of God, I took my family and some friends to a restaurant near our church. Outside the door to the restaurant I met a young man who had just heard my bold affirmation of the joy of giving ourselves away to people in need. He shared a problem he was facing. He needed money for rent. I had some bills folded in my pocket which I had gotten in preparation for a speaking trip I had to go on that evening. I asked the man how much he needed. The amount was exactly how much I had in my pocket—to the penny! "Go and do likewise" echoed in my soul. The man was able to pay his rent and I had to find a place to cash another check before leaving on my trip.[9]

That "look 'em in the eye" involvement and "from the pocket" response is the type exemplified in this story.

The Samaritan did not stop after treating the wounds of the man he found by the roadside. Instead, he elevated the man up onto his own donkey, took him to an inn, and cared for him further. The Samaritan did not stop after delivering the injured man to a place where help was available. Rather, the Samaritan stayed and personally cared for him that night. His personal help only ended when he left the next morning. It was then that the Samaritan paid the innkeeper to continue treatment. The two denarii he gave as payment were coins about the size of our quarter. The equivalent of two days' wages, the money would have been sufficient for a three-week stay at the inn. Included was the promise to return and make good any further expenses incurred. This Samaritan went well beyond mere polite assistance. His actions met every possible need the injured stranger had. To give practical assistance *in person* is part of what it means to express the love of God.

- Love gets personally involved. I will take a hands-on approach with those God places in my path. I will not quickly send them off to others for fixing, but I will do all that I can when I look need in the face.
- Love refuses to stay at a distance. I will not keep my distance, skirting around the need I see up ahead. I will have the courage to get "up close and personal."
- Love gives whatever is needed and all that it can. I will not be stingy when I have enough to meet the need. I will not hold back when it is within my means to give.

We must never underestimate the extent to which God chooses to use us to carry out His will. This brief little story communicates that truth powerfully.

On the street I saw a small girl cold and shivering in a thin dress, with little hope of a decent meal. I became angry and said to God: "Why did you permit this? Why don't you do something about it?" For awhile God said nothing. That night he replied, quite suddenly: "I certainly did something about it. I made you."[10]

Jesus let it be known that to be filled with the love of God requires that we personally and practically give to our neighbor.

6. WE WILL EXPECT GOD'S COINCIDENCES

Rick Tobias is the Executive Director of the Yonge Street Mission in Toronto. Tobias tells of an experience he had on the day after Christmas years ago. It was bitterly cold and he was sick, but he felt he needed to drop by the Mission.

As I climbed the steps to the front door, I noticed a young woman huddled in the corner. Actually, I heard her coughing and gagging before I saw her. She was wrapped in an old sleeping bag and had pulled a toque down over her forehead so that only her eyes peered out from under the rag pile. She was literally shaking from the cold. When she realized my presence she asked me for a cough drop. "I can't seem to stop coughing and my throat hurts like crazy," she said. Fortunately, I was sick enough to be running about with a pocket full of them. So we shared cough drops and I asked her why she wasn't in a warmer place. . . .

Some friends had promised to meet her in the Mission doorway and take her to their squat (an empty building taken over by the homeless). The problem was, they said they would pick her up sometime before dark and it was only noon. . . . I invited her to sit inside the warm building while I tried to stretch a 15-minute task into an hour. Eventually I left for home and she returned to the outside doorway to wait.

When I got home my family looked after my illness.

As I lay on our living room couch one son offered to get me a video while the other brought me a warm blanket. My wife served wonderful Christmas leftovers and I wondered about the woman in the doorway. I wondered if she met her friends and about the quality of care she might or might not receive from them. I wondered if I'd left Jesus in the cold; turned Him away from the only inn available.[11]

We must not miss one of the words in this parable that might seem incidental to the story. In reality it is probably one of the keys in understanding Jesus' point. It is the word that occurs when the priest comes upon the wounded man. Jesus said that the priest "*happened* to be going down the same road." The word Jesus used means "by chance" or "coincidence." As happenstance as this incident may seem, it was a divine appointment. The underlying significance is that although the priest only saw it as a chance encounter, it was an opportunity for him to act out his love for God. "The Lord's timing and staging of life are always perfect for the fulfillment of His plan for us and the people around us. He puts us in situations and with people because of what He wants to do and say though us."[12]

- Love sees opportunities instead of interruptions. As I look at the chance meetings, the unforeseen events, and the unplanned encounters that occur in my life, I must be ready to recognize the hand of God.
- Love receives blessings instead of burdens. I will walk through life with my eyes open. I will never know when I might meet the opportunity God has placed before me to show His love.

Breakthrough Urban Ministry in Chicago was formed in the early 1990s out of a local church. Arloa Sutter, the pastor's wife, was seeing a constant stream of needy people come into the church office. She provided coffee and caring conversation about their needs, but she was convinced that more needed to be done. How could the church help all these homeless people and do so responsibly? The initial answer was very practical and manageable. The church owned a storefront room and from there began to serve lunch every day.

The meeting of this basic need allowed them to see even greater needs. Those needs included giving the homeless an opportunity to maintain their dignity and earn what they were given, as well as providing them with a place to live, job training, and recovery counseling. Through an arrangement with the local Chamber of Commerce, Breakthrough contracted to provide street-cleaning services. This enabled Breakthrough to offer regular jobs to the homeless. Following that came the dedication of the Dwelling Place, a night shelter for thirty men. A social worker, youth outreach coordinator, clinical social worker, and recovery group coordinator were added to the staff. In just five years Breakthrough grew from nothing to minister to more than twenty-two hundred different individuals in 1997. All of that did not really begin with some grand vision for ministry. It began with one woman who showed God's love to the needy people in her path.

That is what the parable of the Good Samaritan is all about. In most cases it will not result in a large ministry as happened with Breakthrough. It will most likely be something that is behind the scenes, quiet, and known only to God. The test of our love for God can come at any time. When it does we must be ready to risk inconvenience. At times we might need to make a conscious choice to sacrifice our safety. Other circumstances may require that we ignore social barriers. Most any need we encounter will demand that we move from emotion to action, giving personal and practical assistance. Every day we should keep our eyes open and expect God's co-incidences. The circumstances may seem coincidental, mere chance, but they are momentous opportunities. If God's love is in us, it will be shown in how we treat the needy ones He puts in our path.

Notes

1. Wiliam Hendriksen, *Exposition of the Gospel According to Luke*, New Testament Commentary (Grand Rapids: Baker, 1978), 591.
2. Norval Geldenhuys, *Commentary on the Gospel of Luke*, The New International Commentary on the New Testament, ed. F. F. Bruce, (1951; reprint, Grand Rapids: Eerdmans, 1979), 311.
3. Walter Liefeld, in *The Expositor's Bible Commentary*, ed. Frank E. Gaebelein, D. A. Carson, Walter W. Wessel, and Walter L. Liefield (Grand Rapids: Zondervan, 1984), 8:943.
4. H. A. Ironside, *Addresses on the Gospel of Luke* (New York: Loizeaux, 1955), 351.
5. Gary Inrig, *The Parables* (Grand Rapids: Discovery House, 1991).
6. Robert O. Boulter, "Reflections on Urban Violence." Personal reflections by the author.
7. William Barclay, *The Daily Study Bible: The Gospel of Luke* (Philadelphia: Westminster, 1956), 142.
8. Flavius Josephus, *The Life and Works of Flavius Josephus*, trans. William Whiston (Philadelphia: Universal, n.d.), 532.
9. Lloyd John Ogilvie, *The Autobiography of God* (Glendale, Calif.: Regal, 1979), 241.
10. Jack Canfield, Mark Victor Hansen, Patty Aubrey, and Nancy Mitchell, eds., *Chicken Soup for the Christian Soul* (Deerfield Beach, Fla.: Health Communications, 1997), 40.
11. Rick Tobias, *The Back Page*, Yonge Street Mission Newsletter, January 1990.
12. Ogilvie, *Autobiography of God*, 235.

chapter three

Knocking on Heaven's Door

"The Friend in Need"
Luke 11:5–13

My in-laws flew in to visit us and rented a big car so we could all ride around town together. There were six of us cruising in a Lincoln Town car. Our youngest daughter, who was then three, sat in the back between her grandmother and mother. This little one has been talking almost since birth. During the ride, she began to direct comments and questions to her grandfather, who was driving. After a few minutes of continuous verbiage from her and no responses from her grandfather, she turned to her mother with a pout.

"Grampa isn't listening to me. How come Grampa won't talk to me? Doesn't Grampa like me? How come he won't say anything?"

We all laughed and explained that her grandfather loves her very much, but he just can't hear very well. When you have owned and operated a sawmill your whole life, deafness comes with the territory. She continued to try to communicate with him, but most of the time he didn't even know she was talking. Finally, she gave up in frustration.

The parable of the friend in need answers some of those same fears and frustrations we have in relation to our heavenly Father. Does God hear me? Is He really listening? If He does hear me, why isn't He answering? Jesus relates this parable to assure us that indeed the Father does hear us and is delighted to answer His children. Before considering the meaning of the parable, it is important that we see the larger context of what Jesus is saying.

> One day Jesus was praying in a certain place. When he finished, one of his disciples said to him, "Lord, teach us to pray, just as John taught his disciples."
> He said to them, "When you pray, say:
>   "'Father,
>   hallowed be your name,
>   your kingdom come.
>   Give us each day our daily bread.
>   Forgive us our sins,
>   for we also forgive everyone who sins against us.
>   And lead us not into temptation.'"
>
> —Luke 11:1–4

While Luke's account of the Lord's Prayer is not the one most familiar to us, it is nonetheless well known. The prayer is prompted by a request from an unspecified disciple. He wants to learn to pray. Notice, he doesn't ask *how* to pray. As G. Campbell Morgan puts it, "This man wanted to know, not the method, but to find the secret of praying; two very different things. There are many people who know how to pray, but they do not pray."[1] What Jesus gives in response is best understood as a model for prayer. This prayer is not for us to memorize only to constantly regurgitate it back to God. It is an excellent practice to pray this specific prayer, yet Jesus did not say to pray these exact words, but to pray *like* this (see Matthew 6:9). This is a pattern for prayer, not a complete substitute. The prayer can be broken down in a variety of ways and in great detail. However, since the prayer is not the focus of this chapter, let me suggest two simple parts into which the prayer can be divided.

PRAY FOR GOD'S HONOR

Real prayer always begins with God. It establishes the kind of God to whom we pray. Prayer reminds us that He is in charge. It is concerned with His interests before our own. It treats Him as holy, sovereign, the One whose purpose is best. Real prayer places God where He belongs and reminds us of our position before Him before it asks a thing. Eugene Peterson comments on this very point. "Prayer means that we deal first with God and then with the world."[2] The first part of this prayer, as well as the prayer recorded in Matthew 6, begins with God. Real prayer adores, worships the Father. Its purpose is to honor Him.

PRAY FOR GOD'S HELP

As much as prayer is to honor God, it is also the means by which we cry to Him for aid. It is crucial that we ask Him for our daily food, even when the cupboard is full and the paycheck sufficient. It is our declaration that we depend upon Him for all things. "The prayer is for our needs, not our greeds."[3] We need Him to supply our daily necessities, forgiveness, and protection. Real prayer asks God for His help, from the ordinary to the extraordinary, the mundane to the miraculous. Real prayer is fused to an understanding that I need God. I can't make it alone—and praise God I don't have to.

This prayer that Jesus models is one that reverences God and declares our dependence. It is following this example that Jesus gives some insight into the privilege of prayer. The main point of the parable and illustration that follows is this: *Do not hesitate to bring your requests to God.* Jesus makes it plain that our heavenly Father delights to answer the prayers of His people. He gives two reasons why.

PRAY—BECAUSE GOD
STANDS READY TO ANSWER YOU

We must be careful not to misunderstand the point of this little parable. Jesus tells this story to demonstrate the contrast in how God responds to us.

> Then he said to them, "Suppose one of you has a friend, and he goes to him at midnight and says, 'Friend, lend me three loaves of bread, because a friend of mine on a journey has come to me, and I have nothing to set before him.'
>
> "Then the one inside answers, 'Don't bother me. The door is already locked, and my children are with me in bed. I can't get up and give you anything.' I tell you, though he will not get up and give him the bread because he is his friend, yet because of the man's boldness he will get up and give him as much as he needs." (Luke 11:5–8)

If you have ever had a knocking at the door in the middle of the night or even a phone call, you can imagine how this man felt. I have had my share of middle-of-the-night disturbances as a pastor and as the chaplain of the fire department. I can't remember any of those instances being good news. Once at two in the morning the phone startled me from sleep. I was asked if this was the home of John Beukema. It actually took me a few seconds to answer, partly because it was 2:00 A.M., and partly because the voice mangled my name so badly. After my affirmative, the caller identified himself as a police officer and asked me to come outside. I asked why. Apparently another officer had found a door open at the church and wanted it locked. I said something like, "That's OK—leave it until morning."

But the officer made it clear that they would not leave me be until I got there and secured the building. Reluctantly I got out of bed, got dressed, walked over to the church, and wandered around until I found the policeman. After making sure there was no one in the building, we discovered that there was no lock on the door and that it had been open like this for quite some time. Finally, I stumbled back to bed and lay awake for two hours. I was glad that we had such a conscientious police force but was not quite as enthused about the loss of sleep.

Jesus paints the picture of a man who disturbs his neighbor at midnight. The reason is far from selfish. He does not come because he wants a late night snack. He does not come because of his own need. He interrupts his neighbor's peaceful night because of someone else's need. A friend has arrived at his home unexpectedly.

It *had* to be unexpected or at least earlier than expected, or the man would have been prepared. It was not uncommon for people at that time to travel in the evening to escape the heat of the day. Perhaps the unexpected friend had decided to keep traveling instead of stopping at an inn. Perhaps there was no reputable place where he could rest. Then he thought, *If I just keep going another few miles I will be at my friend's house. Surely he will take me in.*

Because of the nature of travel in those days, hospitality was a necessity. "Travel was seldom, if ever, for pleasure but rather because of necessity. One never knew when he would be dependent upon the hospitality of others. Therefore a stranger had the right to expect hospitable treatment."[4] Even if the guest arrived after the evening meal was finished, the host should provide something for him. Hospitality was a significant part of the culture. Beyond the expectations of society, it was commanded of the people of God. Because the Israelites themselves had been aliens in a foreign land, God instructed them to care for the aliens among them (Leviticus 19:33; Deuteronomy 10:17–19; 24:17–22).

One of the most flagrant examples of inhospitable behavior is recorded in Judges 19. Godlessness had infected the so-called people of God. A Levite, from whom one might expect spirituality, chased after his missing concubine. She had been unfaithful, but the Levite tracked her down and took her home. On the way, they approached the city of Jebus, which was in enemy hands. Although it was almost dark, they decided not to stay there but to press on to Gibeah. The reason was because Gibeah was a city of Israelites. Certainly they would find a welcome and people who respected the rules of hospitality. "There they stopped to spend the night. They went and sat in the city square, but no one took them into his home for the night" (Judges 19:15). The Levite and his entourage even had their own food and feed for their animals. They only required a roof over their heads, yet no one stepped forward. Finally, an old man who was not even a native extended hospitality to the travelers.

> "You are welcome at my house," the old man said. "Let me supply whatever you need. Only don't spend the night in the square." So he took him into his house and fed his donkeys. After they had washed their feet, they had something to eat and drink. (Judges 19:20–21)

What follows is one of the most revolting passages in the Bible. The wicked men of the city come seeking to have sex with the Levite and end up raping the concubine and abusing her to death. One of the ironies of this story is that the Levite would have been better off with the pagans. He couldn't have been more poorly treated among the aliens in Jebus than he was among the Israelites in Gibeah. The incident was a sign of the moral decay of Israel, a sign that those who claimed God's name were in reality godless.

Such a gross exception highlights the normal expectation of hospitality. Normally, one who arrived at your home was treated with every kindness. So when the friend in the story in Luke arrived unexpectedly, the man was anxious to meet his needs. It was long after the evening meal. There was no bread in the house.

Bread was normally made each day. One didn't bake more than would be eaten because it didn't keep very long. More bread would be baked in the morning, but the problem was what to give this guest tonight. The traveler was tired and hungry. Somehow, the host knew that his neighbor had extra bread. In the tiny community, everyone would know everyone else's business—and the neighbor had a few extra loaves. The man would go and ask his help. He hurried to the house next door and called out to his neighbor. He explained the situation and asked for three loaves of bread.

It does not seem that the neighbor's house was very large. Many commentators describe a one-room home, where everyone is asleep on one mat. Some describe the family huddled around a charcoal fire, surrounded by their livestock. Chickens and goats would have been brought into the house for the night. If that were the case, it is all the easier to imagine why the neighbor would be in no hurry to get up in the middle of the night to answer the door. Imagine the commotion as he tried to step over the children and kids (young goats), hens, and roosters.

Given the construction preferences of that time, it seems more likely that the family was sleeping in an upstairs room. In any case, the neighbor does not want to disturb his sleeping children. To get up from the warmth of his family, find his way to the door, and open it was greatly inconvenient. It was no easy task to pull the wood or metal bar from the hasps and push open the heavy door. So he tells his midnight caller that he won't get up. "Go away. Come back in the morning." But the man will not give up. He keeps calling out, knocking on the door. He will awaken the entire neighborhood. Eventually the neighbor gets up off his cozy mat and stumbles to the door with his arms full of bread. Not only does the man get three loaves, he probably gets every loaf the neighbor has left.

The key word in understanding the point of this parable is the word translated *boldness*. The Greek word Jesus uses, *anaideia*, appears only here in the New Testament. The root of the word refers to modesty and respect. Literally, it means to be without shame, giving the idea of boldness. The word *effrontery* would perhaps be the best choice to describe the meaning of this word. Effrontery is shameless, barefaced audacity. How can this man dare to come at this hour, with this request? He is boldly presuming upon his relationship with his friend and neighbor.

The lesson of this parable is not that if we persist and annoy God long enough, He will answer our prayer. The lesson is one of contrast. If even an imperfect neighbor will undergo inconvenience to answer a request, how much more will our perfect heavenly Father do for us? The man had the audacity to trouble his neighbor because of his need. How ready we should be to shamelessly call upon our heavenly Father to respond to our needs.

Notice how Jesus applied the parable for His disciples. "So I say to you: Ask and it will be given to you; seek and you will find; knock and the door will be opened to you. For everyone who asks receives; he who seeks finds; and to him who knocks, the door will be opened" (Luke 11:9–10). This parable is our encouragement to call upon God. Jesus was confronting our prayerlessness, our lack of willingness to ask God for our needs. If a man would have the audacity to call a neighbor for some bread at midnight, we should have the boldness to call upon God at any time.

Years ago, a fisherman gave me a net loaded with hooks. It was something for which he no longer had a use, and the netted rigging was all balled up and tangled in knots. I decided that I would try to untangle it. I spent a good deal of time fussing with it, hoping to restore that knotted mess to usefulness. After a whole evening of effort, I finally gave up and decided to just cut off the hooks and throw away the line.

It wasn't until I had cut through the net and salvaged a dozen hooks that my wife spoke up. She said, "You know, I could have untangled that." Now that it was too late, my lame efforts had fallen short and I had resorted to destruction. Now she tells me she could have solved my problem. "Why didn't you tell me that before?" I said indignantly. "You didn't ask." That is the very problem that Jesus addresses here. We are too hesitant to call upon our heavenly Father for help. We spend so much time and energy attempting to untangle our problems when the best solution is to ask God.

James wrote of this very issue. He said that prayer-lessness was one of the signs that pleasure is dominating our lives. "You want something but don't get it. You kill and covet, but you cannot have what you want. You quarrel and fight. You do not have, because you do not ask God" (James 4:2). Can there be a more simple solution than to ask God? Yet rather than asking God for our needs and for solutions to our problems, we take action of our own. Lusting, arguing, and fighting takes the place of praying. Yet all the manipulation, scheming, hostility in the world will not bring satisfaction. The charge to God's people is to pray. Simply ask God. One important prayer would be that we desire the right things.

It is by way of application that Jesus encourages us to ask, seek, and knock. There is a sense of persistence here, but it also carries through the idea of shamelessly approaching our heavenly Father with our needs. Yes, prayer is effective. Prayer will be answered. This three-fold charge is certainly arranged according to intensity.

Asking is the basic starting point. To ask is to declare that you have a need. It is a statement of humility that you require something that you cannot achieve on your own.

Seeking goes beyond the request. "They must do everything in their power, to receive what they ask for in prayer."[5]

Finally, comes *knocking.* This is an insistence, a perseverance that keeps on asking and seeking. All three of these words are present imperatives. We could translate them as "keep on asking, keep on seeking, keep on knocking." When Jesus said this was true for everyone, He was referring to those who believe. Everyone who is in a right relationship with God will be answered.

To each of the required commands, a corresponding promise is attached. We will receive, find, and the door will be opened. Taken as a whole, Jesus is encouraging His people to ask God. Pray, because God stands ready to answer. In contrast to the neighbor who answers in exasperation, the Father is anxious to answer our pleas. The time is never inconvenient for the Father. "With God it is never midnight; he never lacks anything; he is never 'bothered' when any humble child approaches him; and he is never taken by surprise."[6] How should I respond to this parable?

- I will resist the temptation to engineer my own answers. Instead, I will make my requests known to God.
- I will delight in the privilege I have to call upon my heavenly Father, marveling over the fact that He stands ready to answer my prayers.
- I will be less concerned with asking for the wrong things than with not asking God anything at all.
- I will pray as passionately for God's honor as I do for God's help.
- I will depend upon my prior relationship with God when I call to Him in time of necessity.
- I will spend less time trying to untangle my own messes and more time asking God.

There is more than a nine-year gap between our two daughters. When the younger one came along, it was as if we were going through it for the first time. One of the women in our church was a midwife. She was anxious to be helpful, and Amy wanted her involved. It was about 2:00 A.M. when the time came. Amy encouraged me to call this friend. She wanted to have her advice, and we also needed someplace for our nine year old to stay while we headed for the hospital.

I remember being petrified of calling the wrong number at that hour, but I dialed. It rang twenty times without an answer. A few minutes later I called again. Another twenty rings with no response. Later we learned that the family, who had just moved into a bigger house, had yet to have more than one phone installed. The one phone they did have was in a downstairs room with their high-school-aged son. Nothing short of a nuclear explosion would have roused him.

I became desperate enough to do something out of the ordinary, that is, to ask someone for help at two in the morning. I phoned a neighbor and got him out of bed. I felt lousy for disturbing him, but he amicably agreed to let our daughter bunk with his daughter for the night. Jesus wants us to know that God always answers the phone. There is never a time when He is not available. He stands at the ready to hear and answer the prayers of His people. We never inconvenience Him, so we must not hesitate to call upon our heavenly Father.

But this parable provokes another question, or at least it should. If the Father simply wants me to ask, what if I ask for the wrong things? Certainly Jesus can't be calling prayer a blank check. This is not a parable endorsing the "name it, claim it" theology, is it? To answer this question, Jesus followed the parable with an illustration. This parabolic illustration gives us the second reason why we should not hesitate to bring our requests to God.

PRAY—BECAUSE GOD KNOWS
HOW TO ANSWER YOU

When I was growing up, our family would often go camping in Maine, Nova Scotia, and other locations on the Atlantic Ocean. During those vacations, we would usually get at least one fried clam dinner. My brother and I loved fried clams. We couldn't get enough of them. In fact, we said as much to our parents. On the few occasions when we were treated to fried clams at dinner, it never seemed to be enough. "You've had plenty, boys," just didn't seem to cut it. "Be thankful for what you have," didn't make much impact either. We still grumbled about not getting enough clams.

One year Dad had heard one complaint too many. He decided to give us our fill of fried clams. I don't know how much it cost him, but he bought two quarts of fried clams from a take-out seafood place. I still remember when he brought those two containers to the car and handed one to each of us. I might have even remarked that it didn't look like very much, but I started eating. We ate our fill, and there were clams left over.

I don't think we looked at another fried clam for a couple of years. Dad wasn't punishing us, but he did teach us a valuable lesson. When you really want something, gorge yourself like a pig. Wait a minute. I don't think that was the lesson. It was more about Dad's knowing what was best for us and his showing us that getting everything you want isn't always so terrific.

Jesus turned to this kind of practical parenting and asked the fathers in the group how they treated their sons. "Which of you fathers, if your son asks for a fish, will give him a snake instead? Or if he asks for an egg, will give him a scorpion? If you then, though you are evil, know how to give good gifts to your children, how much more will your Father in heaven give the Holy Spirit to those who ask him!" (Luke 11:11–13).

The image presented is of a son who asks for something good, something necessary for life. If a fish is requested, a snake is not given. Some manuscripts have bread and stone instead, but this is likely just transferred from Matthew's gospel. In that image, a bread roll may look like a stone, but it is obviously of no use to the needs of a hungry child. That aside, the snake for a fish or the scorpion for an egg are items of danger. No good father would give his child something harmful when the child has some need he is asking his father to fill. A water snake could also be seen as fishlike, and a scorpion could be coiled up in a way that looked similar to an egg. But a good father would not play such tricks on his children. He would not deceive them with danger. Jesus' point was again one of contrast. If sinful, wicked, imperfect humans know how to answer the requests of their children, how much greater is God's ability.

God will know what is best to give in answer to the prayers of His children. God will certainly answer with wisdom. "How much more" probably does not refer to amount, but to the certainty of His response. It is the same sentence construction Jesus uses in the next chapter. "If that is how God clothes the grass of the field, which is here today, and tomorrow is thrown into the fire, how much more will he clothe you, O you of little faith!" (Luke 12:28). The idea was not that God will give us more clothes than He gives to the field adorned with lilies. Jesus was communicating a contrast. If God will clothe the lily of the field in splendid raiment, how much more likely will he refrain from giving us something dangerous when we ask for our daily necessities.

What a joy to think that we can pray with freedom, assured that God knows what is best to give us. Now that we are thinking about our needs—temporal things such as food, shelter, money to pay the bills—Jesus surprises us. Yes, God will give to His children much more readily than an earthly father will. The generous, timely gift that Jesus promises will come from the Father is the Holy Spirit. I love how Alexander MacLaren describes what it means for us to receive the Holy Spirit in answer to our prayers. He says that we will never lack for anything "if we desire that great encyclopedical gift which our loving Father waits to bestow."[7] The Spirit is truly the gift that encompasses all others. All other gifts are included in this one, from A to Z.

- The Holy Spirit secures those who belong to Christ. "And you also were included in Christ when you heard the word of truth, the gospel of your salvation. Having believed, you were marked in him with a seal, the promised Holy Spirit" (Ephesians 1:13).
- The Holy Spirit dwells in those who belong to Christ. "Do you not know that your body is a temple of the Holy Spirit, who is in you, whom you have received from God? You are not your own" (1 Corinthians 6:19).
- The Holy Spirit gifts those who belong to Christ. "Now to each one the manifestation of the Spirit is given for the common good" (1 Corinthians 12:7).
- The Holy Spirit empowers those who belong to Christ. "But you will receive power when the Holy Spirit comes on you; and you will be my witnesses in Jerusalem, and in all Judea and Samaria, and to the ends of the earth" (Acts 1:8).
- The Holy Spirit assists the prayers of those who belong to Christ. "In the same way, the Spirit helps us in our weakness. We do not know what we ought to pray for, but the Spirit himself intercedes for us with groans that words cannot express" (Romans 8:26).

- The Holy Spirit guides those who belong to Christ. "Because those who are led by the Spirit of God are sons of God" (Romans 8:14).
- The Holy Spirit transforms those who belong to Christ. "But the fruit of the Spirit is love, joy, peace, patience, kindness, faithfulness, gentleness and self-control" (Galatians 5:22–23).
- The Holy Spirit fills those who belong to Christ. "Do not get drunk on wine, which leads to debauchery. Instead, be filled with the Spirit" (Ephesians 5:18).

These are just some of the ministries of the Spirit in the lives of God's people. Although the Spirit is a permanent resident in the life of every child of God, we must continually seek to let Him control us. We must rely upon His ability in our lives. There are countless ways that the Spirit can minister to a believer. He can provide power and strength for the pressure we are under. He can offer comfort in the depths of our loneliness. He can give protection in our darkest hours. He can furnish guidance in every decision. He can reveal truth in the midst of error. He can guarantee God's promises in a world of uncertainty. He can produce Christlike qualities in place of our human tendencies. He can come to our aid when we don't know how to pray, or doubt our right to pray, or are unable to pray.

All these things and more are what the Spirit of God can do in us. It is this Spirit that Jesus says is readily available to all who ask. We must ask God for all things, and the greatest request is for the ministry of His Spirit. The Holy Spirit is the all-encompassing gift who makes a life of victory, joy, and blessing possible. Nor do we need to worry about praying amiss because the Father knows exactly how to answer our prayer. Since this is true, there are some actions I must take.

- I will never hesitate to pray because I am not sure of what to ask from God.
- I will trust God to give me what is for my good and for His glory.
- I will make an effort to ask for the ministry of the Holy Spirit in my life above all other requests.

This parable about the friend at midnight and the illustration of a father's gifts teach us much about prayer. We should not hesitate to bring our requests to God because He stands ready to answer us and because He knows how to answer us. This is to be a great encouragement to God's people to simply ask God.

Years ago, I came to pastor a church with very few children and young people. There was a full-time youth pastor, but after nearly four years of ministry, there were virtually no children in the church and no programs for youth or children other than Sunday school.

After the youth pastor was invited to leave, we began a weeknight children's program. The first year was a real challenge. Counting kindergarten through junior high, the number of children attending numbered about a dozen. We labored on through a couple of years, just excited that there was some ministry happening for children. The Lord did bless that tiny effort. A few children and a few parents came to Christ as a result.

Then some of the leaders had a bold idea. They asked if our prayer group would begin to pray that God would bring thirty children into the program. Thirty kids. That number sounded almost astronomical to us. In a church of one hundred and fifty, thirty was a big number. But we began to pray. "God bring thirty boys and girls into this club so that they can hear the good news and grow in their faith. We ask this for Your glory, and Your glory alone."

To our amazement, thirty boys and girls did come that year. In fact, the number didn't stop there. Soon there were fifty. There got to be more children than we could profitably handle. We almost got to the point where we asked God to stop for a while. Within another year it became apparent that for our ministry to continue we would have to enlarge and renovate our facility. A year after that was done, we had more than one hundred children and high school youth involved in the programs.

Those numbers seem small as I consider them now, years later. But the lesson that will not leave me is as plain as it is powerful. All we did was ask God. I realized at that point how seldom I called upon God to act in such a way. How few times I had gotten specific with God and asked Him to do a particular thing for His own glory. There are probably times when I still fail to remember that lesson, but as often as possible I come to the Father like a friend at midnight. How ready He is to answer our requests. How wonderfully He gives what He knows to be for our best. We should not hesitate to bring our requests to God. Much of what we struggle with would be supplied if we would have the audacity to knock on heaven's door.

Notes

1. G. Campbell Morgan, *The Parables and Metaphors of Our Lord* (New York: Revell, 1943), 182.
2. Eugene H. Peterson, *Working the Angles* (Grand Rapids: Eerdmans, 1987), 29.
3. D. A. Carson, in *The Expositor's Bible Commentary,* ed. Frank E. Gaebelein, D. A. Carson, Walter W. Wessel, and Walter L. Liefield (Grand Rapids: Zondervan, 1984), 8:171.

4. R. H. Stein, *The International Standard Bible Encyclopedia,* ed. G. W. Bromiley (Grand Rapids: Eerdmans, 1982), 2:105.
5. Norval Geldenhuys, *Commentary on the Gospel of Luke,* The New International Commentary on the New Testament, ed. F. F. Bruce (1951; reprint, Grand Rapids: Eerdmans, 1979), 325.
6. William Hendriksen, *Exposition of the Gospel According to Luke,* New Testament Commentary (Grand Rapids: Baker, 1978), 614.
7. Alexander MacLaren, *Expositions of Holy Scripture,* vol. 9, *St. Luke* (reprint, Grand Rapids: Baker, 1984), 328.

chapter four

Wise Investments

"The Rich Fool"
Luke 12:13–21

The Collyer boys didn't have to live the way that they did. They had inherited enough money to live comfortably. They were both well educated and could have made a contribution to society. But these two men chose a peculiar path.

They lived in almost total seclusion. They boarded up the windows of their house and padlocked the doors. All their utilities—including water—were shut off. No one was ever seen coming or going from the house. From the outside it appeared empty.

Though the Collyer family had been quite prominent, almost no one in New York society remembered Homer and Langley Collyer by the time World War II ended.

On March 21, 1947, police received an anonymous telephone tip that a man had died inside the boarded-up house. Unable to force their way in through the front door, they entered the house through a second-story window. Inside they found Homer Collyer's corpse on a bed. He had died clutching the February 22, 1920, issue of the

Jewish Morning Journal, though he had been totally blind for years. This macabre scene was set against an equally grotesque backdrop.

It seems the brothers were collectors. They collected everything—especially junk. Their house was crammed full of broken machinery, auto parts, boxes, appliances, folding chairs, musical instruments, rags, assorted odds and ends, and bundles of old newspapers. Virtually all of it was worthless. An enormous mountain of debris blocked the front door; investigators were forced to continue using the upstairs window for weeks while excavators worked to clear a path to the door.

Nearly three weeks later, as workmen were still hauling heaps of refuse away, someone made a grisly discovery. Langley Collyer's body was buried beneath a pile of rubbish some six feet away from where Homer had died. Langley had been crushed to death in a crude booby trap he had built to protect his precious collection from intruders.

The garbage eventually removed from the Collyer house totaled more than 140 tons. No one ever learned why the brothers were stockpiling their pathetic treasure, except an old friend of the family recalled that Langley once said he was saving newspapers so Homer could catch up on his reading if he ever regained his sight.[1]

Homer and Langley are not alone. Many of us are being pulverized by the weight of wrong priorities, crushed by our lust for accumulation, pinned under a mountain of materialism. Those things we pile around us may block our vision of reality. They may cause us to miss a life worth living. Such was the case with a man who was part of a group that crowded around Jesus one day. There were thousands of them, all vying for position. So many were cramped together that Luke writes that they were "trampling on one another" (Luke 12:1). Crowd control became an issue because of a very simple problem. It would be difficult, if not impossible for thousands of people to get close enough to hear one speaker.

Jesus' words were addressed to His disciples, but the throng was seeking to overhear instruction from the Master. With thousands of eavesdroppers surrounding Him, Jesus called His followers to live with confidence because of the value and intimate concern God had for each one of them. But there was one man in this huge crowd who was not satisfied with listening to Jesus' words of wisdom. This man could not keep silent and suddenly blurted out a request, a plea for Jesus' help. "Someone in the crowd said to him, 'Teacher, tell my brother to divide the inheritance with me'" (Luke 12:13). This guy doesn't seem to have paid the slightest attention to what Jesus had been saying. His request was truly apropos of nothing. The man was consumed with discontent over a personal financial situation.

It may seem a little odd that he approaches Jesus with a question about an inheritance. A hint of why he appeals to Jesus is shown when he addresses Him as "teacher." This indicates a position of respect, the position of rabbi. Jesus had no official credentials as a rabbi but was generally considered as such by the common people. A rabbi was expected to be able to investigate and judge ethical matters. Knowledge of the Law qualified a rabbi to render judgment about what was right and fair. This expert knowledge alone became a point of reverence for people, and therefore, rabbis were usually treated with great esteem. So there is a sense of respect shown by bringing this concern to Jesus.

It is strange that the man gives no detail about the case but simply demands that Jesus tell his brother to share. The fact that he makes no mention of the details of the case may indicate that he felt he had a legal right to a part of the inheritance. The Old Testament covers a wide variety of inheritance issues in Numbers 27:8–11; Numbers 36; and Deuteronomy 21:15–17. The man appeals to Jesus' authority and knowledge of the Law to force his brother to comply. "Jesus replied, 'Man, who appointed me a judge or an arbiter between you?' Then he said to them, 'Watch out! Be on your guard against all kinds of greed; a man's life does not consist in the abundance of his possessions'" (Luke 12:14–15).

There were or should have been authorities whose responsibility it was to decide the case. Jesus did not want to interfere with those arbiters. It was possible that this man didn't like the decision already rendered and was looking for Jesus to overturn it. For whatever reason Jesus didn't decide the case but did use the opportunity to speak of this man's true need. Notice that Jesus directed His words to those around Him. He called attention to the man's request and urged the crowd to recognize the real issues. The man was preoccupied with the wrong things, and his desire was greed-based. This man was all worried about what was only money. The disgruntled would-be heir had chosen to pursue money over relationships. He valued a financial debt above things of more intrinsic worth. Jesus called this greed and went on to nail down His point with the parable of the rich fool.

> And he told them this parable: "The ground of a certain rich man produced a good crop. He thought to himself, 'What shall I do? I have no place to store my crops.'
>
> "Then he said, 'This is what I'll do. I will tear down my barns and build bigger ones, and there I will store all my grain and my goods. And I'll say to myself, "You have plenty of good things laid up for many years. Take life easy; eat, drink and be merry."'

"But God said to him, 'You fool! This very night your life will be demanded from you. Then who will get what you have prepared for yourself?'" (Luke 12:16–20)

What is the message of this parable? *Spiritual poverty occurs when our satisfaction depends on accumulation.* Jesus warned that greed robs us of spiritual riches. It would be wise for all of us to evaluate our desires in light of this parable. Jesus' message is surely relevant for the demands and desires of our culture. From this story we can discover the six signs of finding satisfaction in accumulation.

SIGN #1:
OUR SAVING BECOMES HOARDING

Make no mistake; dental hygiene was important in my family when I was growing up. Still, my mother was certain that the toothpaste was disappearing much too quickly. At first when she would discover there was no tube in the drawer by the sink, she just assumed that it had been used up. It was a simple matter to go to the closet and get a new tube—Mom usually bought several at a time. So it took a while for her to get suspicious.

But when buying toothpaste turned from a periodic activity into a weekly necessity, and even then, the demand began to outstrip the supply, Mom and Dad began a covert intelligence operation. They found what they were looking for in my little brother's room, although I'm sure they started in mine. There was a drawer full of toothpaste tubes and bars of soap. He was and is a very clean person, but he wasn't amassing all that stuff to get extra tidy. He was simply collecting. In a simple way and with an innocent face, that is a description of hoarding.

Hoarding is what the rich man was doing. His success, the good crop, brought him to only one consideration. "Where am I going to store all of it?" He thought of no one else whom he could help. There were no other plans beyond stockpiling for his future. The success was not shared or used; it was conserved. The bulging barns would be torn down, and barns more generously proportioned would be erected.

Saving is only dangerous when it develops into hoarding.

- Anything you collect beyond what you can reasonably use becomes hoarding.
- Anything you store needlessly when it is needed by others becomes hoarding.
- Anything you gather that exceeds the foreseen need of preparation is hoarding.
- Anything reserved to force others into need or to raise the value of what you have is hoarding.
- Anything that goes to waste in storage is hoarding.

We must take care that our desire to conserve, our propensity to save, our skill in frugality never grows into greed. For when our saving becomes hoarding, that is a sign that we are finding satisfaction in the wrong place, and the end result will be spiritual poverty.

SIGN #2:
OUR GOAL IS SELF-INDULGENCE

The rich man has a lot of company in North American society. One does not have to look far to find examples of self-indulgence. That is why the following story stands out in contrast and is so newsworthy.

Oseola McCarty, 87, did one thing all her life: laundry. Now she's famous for it—or at least for what she did with $150,000 of the $250,000 she saved by washing the dirty clothes of wealthy bankers and merchants in her hometown of Hattiesburg, Mississippi. For decades she earned 50 cents per load (a week's worth of one family's laundry). But when she finally laid down her old-fashioned washboard—which she always preferred over new-fangled electric washing machines—McCarty decided to ask her banker how much money she had stowed away.

The figure astounded her. Then it set her to thinking. "I had more than what I could use in the bank," she explained to *Christian Reader*, "and I can't carry anything away from here with me, so I thought it was best to give it to some child to get an education."

To the astonishment of school officials, the soft-spoken, never-married laundry woman from a not-so-posh part of town gave $150,000 to the nearby University of Southern Mississippi to help African-American young people attend college. The first recipient is 18-year-old Stephanie Bullock, a freshman at USM, who has already invited Miss McCarty to her 1999 graduation ceremony.

To date, McCarty has been interviewed by Barbara Walters, each of the major network news programs, CNN, *People* magazine . . . and the list goes on. Though she had never traveled out of the South before, McCarty visited the White House, where President Clinton awarded her the Presidential Citizenship Award.

McCarty attends Friendship Baptist Church and reads her Bible every morning and prays on her knees every evening. Discounting the publicity, she says she is simply grateful for the chance to help others gain what she lost: in the sixth grade she was pulled out of school to care for an ailing family member and to help her mother with the laundry.

"It's more blessed to give than to receive," she tells reporters when they ask why she didn't use the money on herself. "I've tried it."[2]

This is the antithesis of the rich man in Jesus' story. This man is characterized by the first person pronoun. He is totally preoccupied with himself. It is not his success that is wrong. The productivity of his land, the prosperity he experiences is not the problem. There is no hint of dishonesty about how he accumulates. The issue is his self-indulgence. Hoarding was a means to an end. The result was to be his long-term enjoyment, a life of ease. He specifies his complete retirement agenda. He will keep on resting, he will catch the early bird special and happy hour, and he will keep on enjoying himself.

This self-centered approach to life and possessions is a threat to spiritual riches. There is nothing wrong with having a good time. Pleasure is not something to be banished from our lives. The problem comes when the focus slips and our purpose is our own pleasure. Gary Inrig wrote, "It is right to enjoy what we have; it is wrong to believe that self-indulgent pleasure is the goal of life."[3] It is this attitude that was condemned by James in his epistle. Speaking to the rich whose money will only bring them misery, James said, "You have lived on earth in luxury and self-indulgence. You have fattened yourselves in the day of slaughter" (James 5:5). A lifestyle made up of soft living and wasteful extravagance is wretched. James pictured the fattening of a calf or chicken, given the best food to gorge itself, only to face the butcher.

Beware if your goal it to live a life of ease in retirement. It is not wrong to plan and save so that you can keep living past sixty-five. Our goal should never be to kick back and do nothing, but to continue to serve God. Whatever our age, we should avoid the tendency to pamper ourselves. God isn't against our enjoying life, but that is different from living in soft luxury and extravagance.

We must evaluate our plans for retirement, our patterns of spending, and our readiness to generosity. We must make sure that our true purpose is not our own pleasure. For if self-indulgence is our goal, that is a sign that we are finding satisfaction in accumulation, and spiritual bankruptcy will be the outcome.

SIGN #3:
OUR PLANNING IS PRESUMPTUOUS

Meet Kristine. She is a type A personality, a driven, high-energy achiever. In her entire life, the only assignment she has ever turned in late occurred when she was twelve, and the dog truly did eat it. Her clothes closet is a thing of beauty. Each garment hangs in the order of date last worn. She does her reading for enrichment during her thirty minutes on the stair stepper each day. She manages her retirement portfolio with skill, constantly evaluating and sculpting her financial future.

Kristin's position with the firm grew, and raises came at expected intervals, culminating in the promotion she deserved. Now it was time to commence with the other phases of her life. First, there would be marriage with Kent. Then at the appropriate time in her career there would be two children, Kaitlin and Kirk. Eventually there would be a house in the suburbs with a big backyard.

Kristine's plans were all reasonable, wholesome, and productive, yet there were a few bridges out on her road to happiness. Kent said no. Kristine hadn't counted on that. A negative response was also forthcoming from Kyle. That hurt because she was really hoping to use the towels already monogrammed with a double *K*. But Kristine finally married Arnie. When Kristine thought the time for children had come, no children came. With the clock ticking, the couple decided to undergo costly fertility procedures. They expended a sizeable portion of their investment capital into the process with no results. It was then that the most unexpected news came. Arnie was downsized into unemployment. A year later, right after Arnie finally got another job, Kristine was unexpectedly expecting. They named her Karny.

Not all of us are type A planners like Kristine. But her story illustrates how much we can assume and how little we can guarantee. The rich man was full of this presumptive planning. He was counting on a long life, and that was something he could in no way guarantee. He had assumed that a future would arrive and that it would be the future he expected.

We all do that to some extent. But this man's mistake was that he did not take God into consideration at all. This exact attitude is forcefully condemned elsewhere in the New Testament.

> Now listen, you who say, "Today or tomorrow we will go to this or that city, spend a year there, carry on business and make money." Why, you do not even know what will happen tomorrow. What is your life? You are a mist that appears for a little while and then vanishes. Instead, you ought to say, "If it is the Lord's will, we will live and do this or that." As it is, you boast and brag. All such boasting is evil." (James 4:13–16)

There is a difference between goal setting and presumptive planning. It is not that we should refuse to make plans and become inactive. Rather, we must watch out for planning as though nothing can stop us. We should daily realize that we are completely dependent upon God. Whatever plans we make may not be within God's purpose. Decisions about the future are wrong when success is assumed and life is taken for granted.

The rich man could not even guarantee that he would be alive the next day. None of us can. We are a wisp of smoke in the wind. We must always take God into consideration; otherwise, we are arrogantly declaring that we are in command of our own destiny.

We must guard our plans from becoming egotistical statements about the future. Assuming the success of our goal, or even the arrival of tomorrow, is a dangerous thing without recognizing the will of God. For if our planning is presumptive, that is a sign that we are finding our satisfaction in the wrong source.

SIGN #4:
OUR OWNERSHIP IS UNQUESTIONED

On the way to setting a new major league baseball season home-run record, Mark McGwire hit a few in Chicago. It was one of those balls that brought about a dispute over ownership. When the baseball left Wrigley Field and landed on the street, there was a crowd waiting. Someone grabbed the ball and everyone piled on. The police had to separate the battlers, and one man got away with the valuable spherical horsehide. Shortly afterwards a lawsuit was filed. The plaintiff charged he was the original possessor of the ball until he was bitten. A bite on his hand was Exhibit A. The defendant claimed he had the ball all along and didn't bite anyone. In the end the suit was settled, and the man who had the ball got to keep the ball.

Think about it. Neither of them had paid anything for that ball, but they each demanded ownership. Neither of them had been involved in the throwing or hitting of the ball, yet they each laid claim. Neither of them had even bought a ticket to the game in which the ball was being used, but they both sought legal possession.

When looked at in that way, both their claims are outrageous. In the screwy world of sports the real owner of the ball might be seen as McGwire. Not the league who purchased the ball, not the owner of the stadium, not the umpire who put it into play, nor the pitcher who served it up would be considered. Two men fought a physical and legal battle over an object that was not theirs.

In a sense, the same is true of this rich man. He experienced success and was preparing to enjoy the many good things he had. But for all his excitement about the gifts, he never remembered that there was also a Giver. He never acknowledged that what he had did not originally come from him, nor did it ultimately belong to him. It was all on loan. "For all practical purposes this man is an atheist."[4] He saw himself as the sole possessor, proprietor. He considered everything he had as his and his alone. There was no consciousness of dependence upon God.

Any one of us can act similarly if we are not careful. That which we have we see as things we have earned. What we achieve has been the result of our work. But as Beyer puts it, "Life is a stewardship, not an ownership."[5] Whatever we have, God has entrusted to us. We have no outright absolute ownership of anything. If and when we fail to recognize that, it is a sign that we are finding our life satisfaction in the accumulation of things and not in God.

SIGN #5:
WE FIND OUR SECURITY IN "STUFF"

Like most of us who live in North America, Ken and Jennie had their share of "stuff." They were two well-educated professionals with a lovely home in a beautiful suburb and their only child in college. They were both in their forties and at the peak of their careers and earning potential.

It was at this time that God called them to an entirely different life. Several church work-treks to Haiti were the catalyst for this change of direction. After months of prayer and counsel, this couple was certain that God wanted them among the poor in Haiti. They keenly felt the great needs of those people, especially the spiritual and economic needs. They also felt the weight of their own materialism. They felt how the conveniences, excesses, and wealth of our culture had the power to distance them from daily dependence upon God.

Unlike Ken and Jennie, most of us don't realize just how easily and deeply entangled we truly are. Sometimes it takes the loss of our stuff for us to recognize our dependence upon possessions. Sometimes our awareness of our dependence upon possessions and convenience may be felt simply by stepping out of our culture and into another for a while. Too many of us never have an experience or an occasion to seriously examine our materialistic attachments.

Ken and Jennie knew the call of God and also knew the grip of dependence upon things rather than God. In response, they sold their home and then the majority of their belongings. Now they live in Haiti. In that place, every drop of water they use must be carried in. They have a small refrigerator, furniture made by a local carpenter, and solar panels for some electricity. Few of the trappings of an upper middle-class North American life remain.

Ken confessed that one of his weaknesses was for fast food. Passing by the myriad of choices readily available in the States was a constant battle. In Haiti the only fast food is an animal you can't catch. For Ken and Jennie there is a stark contrast between what life was and what life is. Certainly, this couple has less of their own in which to trust and more for which to trust God. Stripping away all that stuff would probably be a good thing for any of us. Or, should I say, I am certain that it would be a good thing for me, for it is far too easy for me to have some security in all my stuff. In telling the parable of the rich fool, Jesus spoke directly to this issue.

The rich man founded his security on his wealth. He sought to conserve what he had so that he could guarantee his future. Again, the storage in itself was not wrong. What Jesus took issue with was the man's negligence toward God. The rich man's assurance seemed solely based upon accumulation. Such an attitude was a great spiritual blunder. The Old Testament character Job listed this as one of the sins worthy to be judged. Job declared that having such attractions demonstrates unfaithfulness to God. "If I have put my trust in gold or said to pure gold, 'You are my security,' . . . then these also would be sins to be judged, for I would have been unfaithful to God on high" (Job 31:24, 28).

Wealth gives us the illusion of security. When we find assurance in accumulation, when our possessions are what we depend upon, that is a sign that our satisfaction is misplaced.

SIGN #6:
WE SEE OUR WEALTH AS IN THE MATERIAL

Few authors have sold as many books as novelist John Grisham. His ten novels are worldwide best-sellers. Grisham was interviewed by *Newsweek* magazine about his book *The Testament*. In the novel the main character, Nate, struggles with success and searches for spirituality. When asked if these concerns were his concerns, Grisham said, "The point I was trying to make with Nate was that if you spend your life pursuing money and power, you're going to have a pretty sad life."[6] I agree with Grisham, but Jesus said it first.

All of the rich man's wealth was in the material world. There was no spiritual investment of any kind. Jesus makes that point clear at the conclusion of the parable. "This is how it will be with anyone who stores up things for himself but is not rich toward God" (Luke 12:21). The choice of material possessions over spiritual riches is fatal. Jesus issued a similar warning in Matthew's gospel. "Do not store up for yourself treasures on earth, where moth and rust destroy, and where thieves break in and steal. But store up for yourselves treasures in heaven. . . . For where your treasure is, there your heart will be also" (Matthew 6:19–21).

In the context, Jesus detailed how one stores up wealth in heaven. It is through dependence upon God, prayer and fasting, giving to the needy, loving your enemy, and a host of other heaven-directed activities. Harry Ironside once said, "If you do not have Christ you are miserably poor."[7] Without a knowledge of who Jesus is and what He has done, we have nothing, regardless of how wealthy we may be. Those who claim to be the children of God through faith in Jesus should be spending their time and energy establishing heavenly riches rather than earthly ones. Wherever the majority of our effort is applied and the majority of our "treasure is kept," that is where our affection will be as well. The end of the story for the rich man was that all of his wealth was in the wrong place.

Bunny had it all and yet had nothing. Wealthy and eccentric, he and his wife would drop in for a service at our church a couple times a year. In the process they would notice something that needed doing and offer to purchase it for the church. When Bunny died, I was asked to do the funeral. It was one of those difficult funerals, not made any easier because I was told to refer to him as Bunny all the way through the solemn occasion.

I will never forget watching the expensive casket being lowered into the grave. For it was right then that this realization fully hit me. This man had enjoyed wealth, power, and influence. I had none of those things. But as I looked at his casket, I realized that he had none of the things I enjoyed. He had no satisfaction, hope, security, or peace. When I say that Bunny had everything and nothing, I am contrasting his material and spiritual possessions. Materially he had more than he could ever use in several lifetimes. But he faced death with uncertainty, had a hopeless view of the world and no interest in a personal God. All of his wealth was material.

We must take care that we are not piling up riches in the wrong location. When we can point to our stock portfolio, investment properties, and bank balances more easily than we can identify our spiritual riches, we are on dangerous ground. If the major portion of our wealth is material, that is a sign that we find our satisfaction in accumulation.

Frank LaGrassa is a young man I came to know during the declining health and eventual death of his grandmother. His grandparents were longtime members of our church and actively involved in ministry. Frank is a part of their godly heritage.

This young husband made a decision contrary to conventional wisdom. He had been chosen to take part in a management development program. He completed the first level of training and had a management position that would set the direction of his life for the fore-seeable future. He had seen this as a golden opportunity at first.

But then his mind changed, and he expressed his concerns boldly in a letter to his boss. I received a copy of the letter from his grandfather, who was so proud of what Frank had done. Listen to some of what he wrote to his superior.

> Let me take this opportunity to share with you my ration-ale behind abandoning the prospect of becoming a Man-ager. First and foremost, the enormous time demands placed on Managers make it very difficult (at least for me) to maintain proper perspective on life's priorities. The Lord will always be number one, my wife and family number two, and professional aspirations are third. The minimum fifty-five hours a week required of the position leaves little quality time for church and family.[8]

With those words, Frank stepped away from the pro-gram and became a teacher. Now he and his wife are heavily involved in their church, starting their family, and enjoying a more balanced life. I think Frank made a wise investment.

We must also be concerned about the wisdom of our investments. Jesus warned about the spiritual poverty that results when our satisfaction is based upon our ac-cumulation. Pay attention to the six signs. If my saving becomes hoarding, or self-indulgence is my goal, or my planning is presumptuous, or my ownership is unques-tioned, or my security is stuff, or if my wealth is material, it is a sign of danger. For if any of these things are true, then what I am accumulating is not harmless. Instead, I have begun to make the deadliest of bad investments.

Notes

1. John MacArthur, *Our Sufficiency in Christ* (Dallas: Word, 1991), 37–38.
2. Kevin Dale Miller, "Ordinary Heroes: Oseola McCartney, Washboard of Education," *Christian Reader*, March/April 1996, 81.
3. Gary Inrig, *The Parables* (Grand Rapids: Discovery, 1991), 100.
4. William Hendriksen, *Exposition of the Gospel According to Luke*, New Testament Commentary (Grand Rapids: Baker, 1978), 664.
5. Douglas Beyer, *Parables for Christian Living* (Valley Forge, Pa.: Judson, 1985), 36.
6. Malcolm Jones, "Grisham's Gospel," *Newsweek*, 15 February 1999, 66.
7. H. A. Ironside, *Addresses on the Gospel of Luke* (New York: Loizeaux, 1955), 412.
8. Frank LaGrassa, personal letter, 2 April 1997.

chapter five

Having What It Takes

"The Tower and the Battle"
Luke 14:25–35

I was nearing the end of the final class I needed to complete my master of divinity degree. This was a three-year degree I had raced through in seven years. I was anxious to get on with the rest of my life.

But just a few weeks before graduation I received a note from the registrar. My file was incomplete. I was lacking a couple of items from my original application. I don't remember what they all were, but one of them was a physical examination to give evidence that I was physically able to handle graduate studies. I paid little attention to this. Obviously, I had proven that I was able.

Yet the registrar continued to send me reminders, followed by warnings that I would not graduate. After a personal visit to the registrar's office, I was unable to convince the staff of the pointlessness of this requirement. They told me that I needed a note from a doctor stating that I "have what it takes" to undertake and complete a graduate degree. Now that I was almost out of time, I went to a church member who was a physician and convinced him to supply such a letter. (I'm not sure how valid that was since he was a research anesthesiologist.)

All these years later I still find the whole thing a little silly. I had passed the stringent entrance requirements of a bachelor's degree, sufficient funds, and a pulse. Yet I still needed an independent authority to give assurance that I was capable of doing what I had already done.

Jesus gave all the entrance requirements for following Him right up front. For all those seeking after Him, Jesus forced them to consider, right from the beginning, if they had what it took to be His follower. Jesus never played to the crowd. When He wasn't telling them just how difficult it would be to follow Him, He was chasing crowds away with His hard sayings. Before telling parables that expressed the cost of discipleship, Jesus made some difficult and politically incorrect statements.

> Large crowds were traveling with Jesus, and turning to them he said: "If anyone comes to me and does not hate his father and mother, his wife and children, his brothers and sisters—yes, even his own life—he cannot be my disciple. And anyone who does not carry his cross and follow me cannot be my disciple." (Luke 14:25–27)

Jesus was obviously very popular. Along with His close followers, crowds tagged along. Perhaps they were curiosity seekers, or people who wanted to be part of the excitement, or simply people who wanted to know more about this controversial figure. Whatever their reasons for pursuing Jesus, He didn't let them enjoy a superficial interest for long. As MacLaren puts it, "Christ sought for no recruits under false pretences, but rather discouraged than stimulated light-hearted adhesion."[1]

Years ago, I preached on some other very hard words of Jesus. I remember being concerned that what I had to say would turn people away from Christ, rather than toward Him. The passage was John 6, where Jesus said something that sounds quite revolting. "I tell you the truth, unless you eat the flesh of the Son of Man and drink his blood, you have no life in you" (John 6:53).

In that chapter Jesus spoke much about ingesting His flesh and imbibing His blood. As I preached it, I mentioned how even more horrific this image would be in the minds of His Jewish listeners. For them, drinking blood was an abomination; even eating meat from which the blood hadn't been completely drained was wrong. In some ways, this was shock treatment, which would cause all the hangers-on, the merely curious, to run away. What Jesus was declaring with those words was His indispensability. He presented Himself as the necessity for life, not some luxury or additional blessing. Jesus also used those offending images to illustrate the intensity and intimacy that comes with a relationship with Him. "Whoever eats my flesh and drinks my blood remains in me, and I in him" (John 6:56). I spoke that day of the "Consuming Christ."

When the sermon was finished, I was convinced that I had accomplished exactly what Jesus accomplished when He first said those words. Many disciples quit following Him for good. I remember trudging into my office and somberly contemplating my bright future in a McDonald's uniform. Then there was a knock on my door. I opened it and was surprised to see a college student who was dating one of the girls at church. He took no time with pleasantries. "Pastor, I want this consuming Christ. I don't want to play games, I really want to know Jesus." Right then, this young man committed his life to Jesus Christ. I don't know if anyone was truly chased away by Jesus' words that day, but I do know of one who was drawn to Him.

In similar fashion, Jesus seems to have been thinning out the crowds with these words about hating one's own family and life. He is not a tame or predictable Savior. Rather than being warm and cuddly, Jesus seemed intent on being prickly and demanding. This was a warning shot fired across the bow of popularity, a repellent to the attractiveness of celebrity. His words were a call to whole-hearted devotion. To follow Christ is to choose Him unconditionally over every other loyalty in life. A true disciple has his priorities in the right place. God is first, and if He is not, if there is another attraction, affection, or attachment that comes first, I can't truly be His disciple. "Following Jesus must be the most important thing in our lives, even more than our lives. Nothing must be done that subtracts from that commitment."[2]

We lived in Canada for more than nine years. We loved the church, enjoyed the city of Toronto, and appreciated the country. It was our home. We were able to do everything there except vote in a Canadian election. Voting privileges came with citizenship, and we decided not to become citizens. Our youngest daughter was born in Canada, and she could have dual citizenship, but at that time, no such option was available to us. If we had voted or applied for citizenship in Canada, we would have lost our U.S. citizenship. There could be no division of loyalties. We had to be one or the other.

That is how it is in God's kingdom. You cannot claim citizenship in one kingdom and carry a passport from another. You cannot obtain dual citizenship if you desire to belong to God. Every other loyalty comes second. The hatred Jesus spoke of can be seen as meaning to love less, but we should not let that dull the punch of truth.

There is a sense in which I "hate" all other women except my wife. Through marriage, I have promised to love her above all others. My love for her is so profound, intense, and exclusive that my love for any other woman is hatred by comparison. Jesus went further still by including a hatred for our own lives. That is simply living every day for Him, rather than for my own pleasure and comfort.

This perspective should go even to the point of willingness to die for Christ. A disciple abandons all self-interest and self-preservation for the sake of Jesus. "He who is not willing to die the most hideous death, by crucifixion, for the sake of his love and loyalty to Christ, cannot be His disciple."[3]

This seems quite drastic and harsh to our ears. Such a demanding discipleship is not something often heard today. In fact, it is difficult to read these demands and not wonder if I truly am His disciple. Can I really say that there is no other love in my life that compares to my love for Him? Jesus has no room for a cheap, superficial discipleship. Following Him is an expensive proposition. As Ironside writes, "We cannot serve our Lord Jesus Christ as we should without tremendous cost to ourselves."[4] Jesus is very clear about that tremendous cost.

James Boice has related what happened to a young man who was led to the Lord by the great preacher Donald Grey Barnhouse. The young man was from a prominent family and was serving in the military when he came to Christ. After the war, when it came time for him to return to his upper-class home and family, the new convert mentioned his concerns to Barnhouse, who had led him to Christ.

He talked to Barnhouse about life with his family and expressed fear that he might soon slip back into his old habits. He was afraid that love for parents, brothers, sisters, and friends might turn him from following after Jesus Christ. Barnhouse told him that if he was careful to make public confession of his faith in Christ, he would not have to worry. He would not have to give improper friends up. They would give him up. As a result of this conversation the young man agreed to tell the first ten people of his old set whom he encountered that he had become a Christian.

The soldier went home. Almost immediately—in fact, while he was still on the platform of the suburban station at the end of his return trip—he met a girl whom he had known socially. She was delighted to see him and asked how he was doing. He told her, "The greatest thing that could possibly happen to me has happened." "You're engaged to be married," she exclaimed. "No," he told her. "It's even better than that. I've taken the Lord Jesus Christ as my Savior." The girl's expression froze. She mumbled a few polite words and went on her way.

As short time later, the new Christian met a young man whom he had known before going into the service. "It's good to see you back," he declared. "We'll have some great parties now that you've returned." "I've just become a Christian," the soldier said. He was thinking, *That's two!* Again it was a case of a frozen smile and a quick change of conversation.

After this the same circumstance was repeated with a young couple and with two more old friends. By this time word had got around, and soon some of his friends stopped seeing him. He had become peculiar, religious, and—who knows?—they may even have called him crazy! What had he done? Nothing but confess Christ. The same confession that had aligned him with Christ had separated him from those who did not want Jesus Christ as Savior and who, in fact, did not even want to hear about Him. So it will be for you.[5]

Having declared the great cost of being a real disciple, Jesus gave two parables to further explain that cost. The two parables loosely followed the points Jesus had already made. Using the image of a tower builder and a king preparing for battle, Jesus illustrated the high price of true discipleship: *Following Christ requires all that we have.* The building and the battle each contribute a different obligation for those who desire to be disciples of Jesus Christ.

DISCIPLES MUST BE READY
TO FINISH WHAT THEY START

"Suppose one of you wants to build a tower. Will he not first sit down and estimate the cost to see if he has enough money to complete it? For if he lays the foundation and is not able to finish it, everyone who sees it will ridicule him, saying, 'This fellow began to build and was not able to finish'" (Luke 14:28–30).

My parents used to own a home in the country. Surrounded by past and present farms, neighbors were few and far between. One neighbor who moved in while my parents lived there was a man from the big city. He had retired early and was trying his hand at country life. I don't know exactly what Al was hoping to accomplish, but he seemed to dabble in a few things—horses, livestock, farming. Then one day he began to build another barn. There was an old barn already in use across the road. But Al began to build this barn on the same side of the road as his house. Strangely, it was pretty far away and up on a hill.

The neighbors watched with interest. The slab was poured for the floor, the main beams were in place, and eventually a roof took shape. Somewhere along the way progress screeched to a halt. Since the barn sat on a high point, it was more noticeable than the house. Whenever you drove down the road, your eye would be drawn to that partly finished structure. It loomed large over the landscape. A huge, skeleton of a building. Quietly, it became known as "Al's Folly."

It was bad enough that the building was begun in such an odd place. It was a downright scandal that it remained incomplete. Speculation ran wild. Did Al run out of money? Did Al reconsider the location of his barn? Did Al stop construction because he was considering turning the barn into a house and the house into a barn? Maybe Al was just a city slicker who was in over his head.

Eventually Al finished the roof of the barn and began to store things underneath the structure. Now when you drove down the road and stared at the barn, you could see everything sitting in storage underneath the roof. Perhaps that was all Al ever intended to build. Perhaps he just wanted a really tall pole-barn. Perhaps Al was broke. "Al's Folly" was part of the idle talk of the neighborhood for quite some time.

The tower Jesus mentioned was a tall structure used for defense, protection, or attack. Usually it was part of the city wall. It was the same type of building Jesus referred to in Luke 13:4. There, a specific tower collapsed and eighteen people were killed. Such construction would be obvious and a significant undertaking. A responsible person would sit down and count the cost before he began to build. Jesus said it was simply common sense not to start building unless you knew that you had what it took to finish the project. To begin to build and then quit would turn you into the community joke. Scorn and ridicule would be justly deserved. Consider the cost. Look before you leap. What specific implications for discipleship are presented through this parable? Jesus demonstrates that to be a true disciple, you must finish what you start.

Finishing Demands that
You Consider the Possible Cost

What does Jesus mean when He talks about sitting down and estimating the cost? The word translated *estimate* has the root from the word meaning pebble. Since at one time pebbles were used as an instrument for counting, the verb was used to describe calculating and counting.[6] Do we have the resources necessary to finish? Are we willing to commit all that we have to finish? Are we ready to give whatever it takes?

That is the real question. We *don't* have all that it takes, but we need to be willing to give, to sacrifice all that we have to the goal. Jesus began by giving an idea of just how costly following Him could be. The cost may not merely involve resources of money, time, and energy. The most expensive consequence may be relationships. Ironside relates this account of what it cost a young woman to follow Christ.

I remember a dear, young Jewish girl who came to the Lord Jesus Christ and was saved. When she was to be baptized her Jewish mother, who loved her tenderly, said in a paroxysm of anger, "Oh, my daughter, do you hate your mother so much that you would go down to that church and be baptized?" The daughter insisted that she loved her mother, but that she loved Christ more. Her mother said, "You do not love me, or you would never be baptized. You hate me; that is why you are being baptized." The daughter knew that faithfulness demanded that she turn away from her dear mother as though she hated her, although it was almost more than she could endure.[7]

To understand that high price going in was something Jesus did not want to hide from those seeking to be disciples. It is not that we should be arrogantly sure that we will finish before we can safely begin. It is that we have understood how much it will take to finish. We must have our eyes opened to the demands of discipleship, the cost of following Christ. None of us can make it on our own in any event. What is required is a willingness to give all we have to that goal.

Finishing Demands that You Make Progress

"Oh, the Church is full of these abortive Christians; ruins from their beginning, standing gaunt and windowless, the ground-plan a great palace, the reality a hovel that has not risen a foot for the last ten years."[8] In a sense, we are all incomplete until we are face-to-face with Christ. It is not our incompleteness that should alarm us. It is a total lack of progress, an absence of aspiration, a lack of any forward movement whatsoever that should cause us concern. Are we any different today than we were five years ago? That is a question we should keep in our minds as we follow Christ. Are we growing in the grace in which we claim to live? It is not that we will grow beyond struggles, will never have the same temptations or failings. Rather, it is that we are allowing the Spirit of God to shape us, to make us more like Christ.

Like most families with children, we've have had growth charts and markings on the wall to show our kids how they've grown. After a while, such measurements are no longer relevant because we stop growing. One ongoing measurement that is still unfortunately relevant in my life is the bathroom scale. But unlike the growth in height and weight, which does stop or should stop, our progress in Christ should not stop. Laying the foundation—beginning to follow Christ—is an exciting, joyous occasion, but it cannot stop there. I liken it to the sense of accomplishment I have felt when getting a baby to burp. You feed, you wait, you pat, you coax, and then finally there is success. For some reason, it isn't quite the same emotion you feel when Aunt Mildred belches in the restaurant.

Finishing Demands More than a Good Beginning

I have never been to a racetrack in my life. I have never purchased a lottery ticket, or bet money on anything in all my years. I say that so you'll know where I'm coming from in this story. When I was in high school, a local grocery store had some sort of promotion that involved horse racing. Every purchase included a ticket with the name of a horse and the number of the race the next Saturday. They would then televise races that had been previously run, and if your horse won, you were awarded some sort of prize.

I remember seeing the race on TV. My mother had recently gone shopping, and I found the ticket she'd received. At the bell, "my horse" took the lead. Around the first turn, he was pulling away from the pack. I got excited. Around the next turn, there were a couple of horses getting closer, but "my horse" was still well in the lead. Down the stretch he was still leading. My palms were sweaty. My heart was thumping. Suddenly "my horse" looked like a candidate for the glue factory. Within yards of the finish, he was passed. "My horse" finished fourth.

Disappointed, but hopeful at how close I had come, I began to sneak off with Mom's grocery slips every Saturday. Every Saturday, "my horse" would take the lead.

Every Saturday I lost. After a few weeks of that, I realized that the grocery store found races like this and printed a million tickets with the lead horse's name, the horse that never won. I quit my racing habit cold turkey.

It is not as important how you start out as how you finish. A great beginning means nothing if there is no ending. "Many a man and woman leaves the starting-point with a rush, as if they were going to be at the goal presently, and before they have run fifty yards turn aside and quietly walk out of the course."[9] As in the parable of the soils ("The Sower and the Seed," discussed in chapter 1), these people are the seed that falls on the rocky soil. The seed springs up and there is an emotional response, but it withers under the heat of temptation and trouble. This is an impulsive commitment that will not last. Jesus did not want flashes in the pan, but those willing to walk through flames for Him. "You want to be My disciple?" Jesus asks. "Then be ready to do whatever it takes to finish what you start."

DISCIPLES MUST BE
READY TO SACRIFICE EVERYTHING

"Or suppose a king is about to go to war against another king. Will he not first sit down and consider whether he is able with ten thousand men to oppose the one coming against him with twenty thousand? If he is not able, he will send a delegation while the other is still a long way off and will ask for terms of peace" (Luke 14:31–32).

This mention of the king and a battle avoided does not easily mesh with the image of the builder. In fact, there are all kinds of applications and interpretations that could be gathered from this scene. Commentators have at times drawn opposite conclusions from the same words. The obvious similarity between the king and the builder is that both are seen as estimating to determine if they have what it takes to complete the project.

Yet that cannot be the greatest point that Jesus is making. Notice how Jesus Himself summed up the point of the parable. "In the same way, any of you who does not give up everything he has cannot be my disciple" (Luke 14:33). Disciples must be willing to pay whatever it costs, to sacrifice whatever is necessary. To hold back something, to be conservative with what we have, not to risk it all, means we cannot be His disciples.

Sacrificing Everything Means Accepting the Costs

Elizabeth Dirks is one of my heroes. She is an example to me of a disciple ready to sacrifice it all for Christ. I first encountered Elizabeth years ago in the pages of a book on the history of the Reformation. She was part of a radical movement that was sweeping the church in the 1500s. The Anabaptists had strong convictions that brought them into dispute with other Protestants and Catholics alike. Among other things, they believed that only confessing believers should be baptized, not infants. They believed one could not be born into the church but must become a believer and be baptized to become part of the church. They believed that the only standard for their lives should be the New Testament. The differences were such that Anabaptists became the targets of bitter persecution.

Elizabeth was arrested on January 15, 1549. Taken to prison between two guards, she was brought before the council for interrogation. They threatened Elizabeth to get her to reveal the names of those she had taught, the name of her teachers, and other friends. "Elizabeth: 'Oh, no, my lords, let me in peace with this, but interrogate me concerning my faith, which I will gladly tell you.' Lords: 'We shall make you so afraid that you will tell us.' Elizabeth: 'I hope through the grace of God that he will keep my tongue, so that I shall not become a traitoress, and deliver my brother into death.'"[10]

Elizabeth responded to each accusation with graciousness, Scripture, and firm belief. She refused to back away from her faith and so was taken to the torture chamber. Hans, the executioner began his work. "He applied the thumbscrew to her thumbs and forefingers, so that the blood squirted out at the nails. Elizabeth said, 'Oh! I cannot endure it any longer.' The lords said, 'Confess, and we will relieve your pain.' But she cried to the Lord her God: 'Help me, O Lord, thy poor handmaiden! For thou art a helper in time of need.'"[11]

The council told her to stop calling out to God and offered to take away the pain if she would only confess. But the Lord had answered her cry, and Elizabeth told them she no longer felt the least pain. "Lords: 'Will you not yet confess?' Elizabeth: 'No, my lords.' They then applied the screws to her shins, one on each. She said: 'O my lords, do not put me to shame; for never a man touched my bare body.' The Procurator-General said, 'Miss Elizabeth, we shall not treat you dishonourably.' She then fainted away."[12]

Two months later Elizabeth Dirks was condemned to death. I marvel at this woman's faith in Christ. She had counted the cost of discipleship and was willing to sacrifice her life. Most of us will not have the opportunity, but a disciple must be ready.

Consider the king Jesus described. He was different from the builder in that he didn't have a choice. The builder should have counted the cost before beginning, but the king was faced with an approaching enemy. He only had two options: fight or make peace. The estimation was simple. Can an army of ten thousand repel an army of twenty thousand? The word *able* here refers to being "capable," being "in position" to win. If the king saw this as a no-win situation, then he would look to broker a peace agreement. Jesus couldn't have been commending surrender to the enemy. His point couldn't have been "If you don't think you can win, better to give up early than to lose." This parable was in the context of describing the type of sacrifice required to be His disciple.

Sacrificing Everything Means Going Against the Odds

The Bible is full of instances where God calls someone to go against the odds. David against Goliath. Israel against Jericho. Gideon against Midian. God delights in using what seems inadequate, what appears insufficient to accomplish His purposes. That way the glory goes to Him. The little shepherd boy with a sling goes against a giant of a man who is an armed and experienced warrior. The ragtag group of refugees marches around a heavily fortified city inhabited by large, powerful people. The cowering farmer with low self-esteem is called to gather an army to face an invader with 135,000 soldiers. By any human accounting victory appears impossible.

In the case of Gideon, the cowering farmer, God made His point abundantly obvious. Flush with renewed confidence in God, Gideon called together an army of his people. Thirty-two thousand answered the sound of the trumpet. This was an encouraging response, even though these were farmers with few weapons and no training. God assured Gideon of victory and then did the incomprehensible. Although this motley crew of Israelites was outnumbered four to one, God told Gideon his army was too big. The cowards were invited to leave, and the odds went to thirteen to one. God sifted and tested the volunteers who stayed, and only three hundred soldiers were left.

At first, victory was a calculated risk, then it became improbable, until with only three hundred it appeared impossible. God wanted a group so inadequate that only He could have the glory. With God, all things are possible, and without Him we can do nothing. To be His disciple is to be willing to go against the odds and face any opposition.

Sacrifice Everything Means Giving Up Even Life Itself

The king is not willing to fight a battle he cannot surely win. He is not willing to risk the lives of his troops and ultimately his own life when the odds are against him. The application Jesus gave concerned a willingness to give up everything for Him. The king was not willing to risk his army, his kingdom, or his life against those overwhelming odds, so he quit. But in order to win, he had to risk it all. The disciple has to say good-bye, cast aside, leave behind everything for Christ.

There is a true story of a little boy whose sister needed a blood transfusion. The doctor explained that she had the same disease the boy had recovered from two years earlier. Her only chance of recovery was a transfusion from someone who had previously conquered the disease. Since the two children had the same rare blood type, the boy was an ideal donor.

"Would you give your blood to Mary?" the doctor asked.

Johnny hesitated. His lower lip started to tremble. Then he smiled and said, "Sure, for my sister."

Soon the two children were wheeled into the hospital room. Mary, pale and thin. Johnny, robust and healthy.

Neither spoke, but when their eyes met, Johnny grinned. As the nurse inserted the needle into his arm, Johnny's smile faded. He watched the blood flow through the tube. With the ordeal almost over, Johnny's voice, slightly shaky, broke the silence.

"Doctor, when do I die?"[13]

Jesus wants us better informed than that little boy. He alerts us from the beginning that the cost is high, and our lives may be required. But that willingness and readiness to sacrifice it all for Jesus is the stuff of a disciple. We must have a constant, daily perspective of abandonment toward everything that we have and hold dear, even our own lives.

With these parables, Jesus was not encouraging us to estimate our resources and our willingness to sacrifice so that we can back out gracefully. He was alerting us to the high cost of discipleship so that we will give it all we have. A commentary from the last century says it this way: "The tower must be built; the strife must be striven; the kingdom of heaven must at any price and above all be sought."[14] Unless that is our perspective, we will be of little use to the Master, and that is why Jesus concluded with these words. "Salt is good, but if it loses its saltiness, how can it be made salty again? It is fit neither for the soil nor for the manure pile; it is thrown out. He who has ears to hear, let him hear" (Luke 14:34–35).

If we want to be disciples, then we must be willing to give it all we have. We must be like the builder who commits all his resources to finish what he has started. We must be like the king who is willing to go against the odds and sacrifice everything. If we are not, then we are as worthless and ineffective as stale salt. "In the economy of God uselessness invites disaster."[15] Unless we are willing to be His disciple, we will never know the highest happiness that can be found in this life or in the life to come. We will never discover a life worth living.

Notes

1. Alexander MacLaren, *Expositions of Holy Scripture,* vol. 9, *St. Luke* (reprint, Grand Rapids: Baker, 1984), 38.
2. James Montgomery Boice, *Christ's Call to Discipleship* (Chicago: Moody, 1986), 120.
3. Norval Geldenhuys, *Commentary on the Gospel of Luke,* The New International Commentary on the New Testament, ed. F. F. Bruce (1951; reprint, Grand Rapids: Eerdmans, 1979), 398.
4. H. A. Ironside, *Addresses on the Gospel of Luke* (New York: Loizeaux, 1955), 475.
5. Boice, *Christ's Call to Discipleship,* 122–23.
6. William Hendriksen, *Exposition of the Gospel According to Luke,* New Testament Commentary (Grand Rapids: Baker, 1978), 739.
7. Ironside, *Addresses on the Gospel of Luke,* 477.
8. MacLaren, *St. Luke,* 45.
9. Ibid.
10. Hans J. Hillerbrand, *The Reformation* (Grand Rapids: Baker, 1981), 243.
11. Ibid., 244.
12. Ibid.
13. David C. Needham, *Stories for the Heart* (Portland, Oreg.: Multnomah, 1987), 128.
14. J. J. Van Oosterzee, *A Commentary on the Holy Scriptures: The Gospel According to Luke,* trans. Philip Schaff and Charles Starbuck (New York: Charles Scribner, 1867), 2:232.
15. William Barclay, *The Daily Study Bible: The Gospel of Luke* (Philadelphia: Westminster, 1956), 205.

chapter six

God's
Open
Arms

"The Lost Things"
Luke 15

I love to have a good time and make people laugh, but frankly, I don't think that I really know how to party. When I hear the word *party,* it evokes an image of dancing, frivolity, and a level of celebration with which I haven't had much experience. It must be my Baptist background. Consider these examples.

My high school graduation party consisted of three aunts and uncles, a great-aunt, and a second cousin. The high point of the event was that my mom made two kinds of cheesecake.

When my wife and I were married, we had two receptions. The first reception was with about five hundred people and held at the church. The other reception was a dinner for about seventy and held at a nearby hotel. Both receptions were very nice, but neither was what I would call a party. My dad was a Baptist pastor and my father-in-law was a deacon in that very church. Our party was reserved and polite and everything was under control. *Raucous* is not a word that comes to mind when Baptists plan a party.

Recently I turned forty. At the time, I was on a work trek with a dozen other people. After a hard day's work, they all surprised me with funny cards and a cake. The pinnacle of celebration came when I was taken into the backyard and surrounded by all my fellow workers. Everyone was supplied with water balloons and then invited to hurl them at me. It was a painful and damp birthday.

Those examples should make it clear that I am party impaired. Perhaps you can understand why it takes some imagination for me to picture God partying. That may be difficult for you too. It may even seem sacrilegious. But if you listen to some of the most familiar stories Jesus ever told, He speaks about times when God celebrates.

Look first at the setting in which Jesus related the parable. "Now the tax collectors and 'sinners' were all gathering around to hear him. But the Pharisees and the teachers of the law muttered, 'This man welcomes sinners and eats with them.' Then Jesus told them this parable" (Luke 15:1–3). It was outrageous behavior for Jesus to hang with these kinds of people. Tax collectors were detested because many were greedy, conniving, and dishonest swindlers. The other group that came to listen to Jesus was described as "sinners." The word is in quotes because it was not a specific group of people. Rather, it was a broad description of those regarded as inferior by the upstanding citizens. *Sinner* was a general word for those who missed the mark. These people weren't the outwardly religious, but the misfits, those who were seen as failures and immoral in comparison with others. They were the crowd that was obviously wicked, at least to the religious. They were people who had been perpetrators of various vices or crimes. Decent people did not associate with such trash.

But when these tax collectors and "sinners" crowded around Jesus, He treated them all with dignity and value. He responded to the social outcasts as if they were equal to the religious and social elite. Jesus wasn't afraid of contaminating Himself or His reputation, and His lack of discretion seemed scandalous to the religious leaders.

Actually, it was the so-called misfits who were the ones most attentive to Jesus throughout His ministry. "The kind of people who were attracted to Jesus in his lifetime were not the religious and social sophisticates, but rather those who had made a mess of their lives."[1] In response to the muttered complaints of those who disapproved, Jesus tells three stories. Verse 3 calls it a parable, singular. It is only one parable with three parts. However, the three stories will not placate the disgruntled ones listening to Jesus. For, in effect, Jesus said, "It's far worse than you think. I don't only *eat* with sinners, I go out *looking* for them, bring them home, and party!" That is the beautiful lesson of this chapter.

GOD CELEBRATES OVER
EVERY REPENTANT SINNER FOUND

The first story is of the shepherd who values even one stray member of his flock.

> "Suppose one of you has a hundred sheep and loses one of them. Does he not leave the ninety-nine in the open country and go after the lost sheep until he finds it? And when he finds it, he joyfully puts it on his shoulders and goes home. Then he calls his friends and neighbors together and says, 'Rejoice with me; I have found my lost sheep.' I

tell you that in the same way there will be more rejoicing in heaven over one sinner who repents than over ninety-nine righteous persons who do not need to repent." (Luke 15:4–7)

The shepherd gives every effort until the sheep is found, and it is only right and fitting that he does so. "His search would not be half-hearted, not merely a token search. No, he would leave behind the ninety-nine and look for that one lost sheep *until* he finds it!"[2] This concern of the shepherd for one lost lamb is seen in an experience H. A. Ironside relates.

Years ago I was staying with friends who had a great sheep ranch, and one evening we were awaiting supper until the husband came home. We expected him to arrive about six o'clock, but he was late.

When he came into the house, he said to his wife, "My dear, I shall have to drink a cup of coffee and eat only a snack tonight, for as I came from the station I heard the bleating of a lost lamb, and I must hurry and find it before the coyotes or rattlesnakes get it."

I asked if I might go with him, and he consented. I was amazed to see that man's interest in one lost lamb. He and a friend had more than five thousand sheep and literally thousands of lambs; and yet that one lost lamb had such a place in his heart that he could not resist going out in the night to find it.

I said, as we went along a narrow trail, "You have so many sheep and lambs, I wonder why you are so much concerned about one."

He said, "I would not be able to sleep tonight for thinking about that little lamb out in the wilderness, and perhaps torn into pieces by the coyotes or bitten by a rattler."

He called out as we went along the trail, "Bah-h-h, bah-h-h, bah-h-h." He listened eagerly for an answer. At last we heard, from far down in the canyon among the thick brush, a little voice crying, "Baa . . . baa . . . baa."

My friend answered with a loud "Bah-h-h, bah-h-h, bah-h-h, bah."

He said, "There it is. You stay here; I'll go down and get it."

And down he went, holding on to his flashlight; and when he got to the bottom he shouted back, "I have it; it is all right!" We went home rejoicing together.[3]

Such is the delight and the desire of the shepherd for each one in his flock. When he does find the lost lamb, the shepherd doesn't punish it, nor does he complain about all the inconvenience and sacrifice. The finding is an occasion of great joy and a significant cause for celebration. "The focus of the parable is on the effort expended and the joy experienced because of just one lost and found sheep."[4]

The implication is that there should be a correlative celebration on earth for a repentant sinner. Heaven itself celebrates over every sinner who repents. But there is no party for the "righteous." There is little or no rejoicing in the halls of heaven for those who do not need to repent. The righteous persons Jesus referred to were not those who were considered righteous by God, but those who had no obvious or flagrant sins to confess. They were the religious, the social upper crust, and the morally upright who saw nothing in themselves over which to repent. They were the ones who thought they had it all together, and there was no joy among them or for them. In contrast, there was much joy for the wayward one who had wandered off into dangerous separation from the flock and then was been brought back.

Jesus continued the threefold parable with another lost item.

"Or suppose a woman has ten silver coins and loses one. Does she not light a lamp, sweep the house and search carefully until she finds it? And when she finds it, she calls her friends and neighbors together and says, 'Rejoice with me; I have found my lost coin.' In the same way, I tell you, there is rejoicing in the presence of the angels of God over one sinner who repents." (Luke 15:8–10)

The coin in question was worth the wages of an entire workday. The story implied that these coins were all she had. There was no question that she would search long and hard. Her poor home would only have a dirt floor. It would not be easy to find this coin. "In this second parable the focus is more on the strenuous effort of the woman in looking for what was lost."[5] She swept every nook and cranny of the house. Her search was thorough and tireless until the treasured piece was found. This one coin was valuable and worth all of the effort expended.

I remember as a little boy being at the beach with my parents and one of my mother's sisters and her husband. I remember the panic that occurred when it was discovered that my aunt had lost her diamond ring. All the adults were searching frantically. You can imagine the "needle in a haystack" feeling of hunting for something that small on a beach full of sand. My father prayed that God would help him find it. Suddenly, his prayer was answered. Somehow in the middle of all that sand and surf, my dad found the ring, and he praised God. In fact, everyone was overjoyed and did a lot of praising. That is the picture here. The rediscovered coin is cause for a party. It is a time to invite others to share the joy. Jesus again draws the connection to the heavenly celebration. "God, who has his dwelling in the presence of the angels, seeks sinners, and rejoices over even one of them who repents or is converted."[6]

Jesus completed the three-part parable with the vivid story of a lost son. This prodigal did not wander off like the lamb, and he was not accidentally lost like the coin. He willfully left home.

"There was a man who had two sons. The younger one said to his father, 'Father, give me my share of the estate.' So he divided his property between them.

"Not long after that, the younger son got together all he had, set off for a distant country and there squandered his wealth in wild living. After he had spent everything, there was a severe famine in that whole country, and he began to be in need. So he went and hired himself out to a citizen of that country, who sent him to his fields to feed pigs. He longed to fill his stomach with the pods that the pigs were eating, but no one gave him anything.

"When he came to his senses, he said, 'How many of my father's hired men have food to spare, and here I am starving to death! I will set out and go back to my father and say to him: Father, I have sinned against heaven and against you. I am no longer worthy to be called your son; make me like one of your hired men.' So he got up and went to his father.

"But while he was still a long way off, his father saw him and was filled with compassion for him; he ran to his son, threw his arms around him and kissed him.

"The son said to him, 'Father, I have sinned against heaven and against you. I am no longer worthy to be called your son.'

"But the father said to his servants, 'Quick! Bring the best robe and put it on him. Put a ring on his finger and sandals on his feet. Bring the fattened calf and kill it. Let's have a feast and celebrate. For this son of mine was dead and is alive again; he was lost and is found.' So they began to celebrate." (Luke 15:11–24)

The request this son made was not a polite one. In so many words he said, "Dad, I can't wait until you're dead." The son's share of the estate would not ordinarily come to him until his father had passed away. This was certainly a disrespectful and thoughtless demand. When the father did die, one-third of the estate would belong to this second son. The firstborn son had rights greater than those of the younger son. This birthright of the firstborn was what Jacob cornered his older brother Esau into selling him. The conniving Jacob offered a pot of tasty stew in return for the birthright, and the famished Esau foolishly accepted the bargain. In a material sense, the birthright likely was a double portion of the inheritance. That was what is required for the actual firstborn son in multiple marriages in order to prevent favoritism.

> If a man has two wives, and he loves one but not the other, and both bear him sons but the firstborn is the son of the wife he does not love, when he wills his property to his sons, he must not give the rights of the firstborn to the son of the wife he loves in preference to his actual firstborn, the son of the wife he does not love. He must acknowledge the son of his unloved wife as the firstborn by giving him a double share of all he has. That son is the first sign of his father's strength. The right of the firstborn belongs to him. (Deuteronomy 21:15–17)

Eventually, one-third of the father's possessions would have been his, but the impetuous young man wanted his right away. However long it took his father to liquidate his holdings or to arrange his business so that he could honor the request Jesus did not mention. When the second son collected his early inheritance, he got as far away as he could. He went to a distant country so that he could live as he pleased. Dad would be unable to see how he spent the inheritance.

And spend he did. There is no real indication of what the money was spent on, just that it was gone in a hurry. The word *squandered* means to scatter, to waste, to throw up into the air. We don't know if it was wine, women, and song, or leisure, laughter, and lending. "He spent money right and left until there was nothing left."[7]

At that point, when he had nothing left, things got hard for everyone, as a famine gripped the land. Desperate to stay alive, he took the lowest job imaginable. "To the Jew especially the feeding of swine was a most repulsive occupation."[8] "He accept[ed] the most humiliating and repulsive form of servile labour—[herding] the swine of one of the citizens of the distant country."[9] But even that got him nothing. Destitute and starving, he came to himself and woke up to the reality of what he had done and what he needed to do. He realized just how foolish he had been. The son prepared to return home and rehearsed a speech to give to his father. It sounds as if he truly repented. He called his actions sin against God and his father. He was willing to go back even as a lowly day laborer.

So the young man began the long journey back. He was still a far distance away when his father saw him. This is a key element in the story. The boy did not make it all the way home; the father spotted him first. The father was the one searching. Dad never stopped looking for his son. Just like the lost lamb and the lost coin, this son was the subject of great concern. Full of love and pity, the father ran to the boy. This itself was something out of the ordinary. "Traditional Middle Easterners, wearing long robes, do not run in public. To do so is deeply humiliating."[10] When he reached his son, there was no expression of rebuke, no mention of the expense and inconvenience. Not even any questions about where the boy had been or what had happened to the inheritance. All that occurred was simply exuberant joy and demonstrative love, a hug and a kiss.

Finally, the son got out some words. He didn't say his whole speech, just that he had sinned and wasn't worthy to be a son. But Dad's reaction was so opposite of the expected. No punishment, no payback or recrimination of any kind. He did not ground his son for a year, set up a repayment plan, garnish his allowance, or even express hurt; there was just celebration. The best robe, a ring, sandals, a fat calf to feast on. It was party time. This son was dead and lost, but now he was alive and found.

Wait a minute! That's what the father said. "My lost son has been found." Who found him? Hadn't he come home on his own? Wasn't it the son who came to his senses and returned? "In the father's perceptions, the Prodigal was still lost and dead at the edge of the village."[11] The father was looking for him, longing for him, waiting for him all the time.

The Sunday school teacher held the rapt attention of her first grade class as she told the story of the Prodigal Son. She described in great detail the wonderful party and sumptuous feast that the father gave for the son he found. Then she said, "But there was one who wasn't happy about all this celebration. There was one who didn't want to attend the party. Who was that?" One little boy raised his hand and said, "I think it was the fatted calf."[12] While that was true enough, there was another who was less than pleased about the return of the lost son and the subsequent celebration.

"Meanwhile, the older son was in the field. When he came near the house, he heard music and dancing. So he called one of the servants and asked him what was going on. 'Your brother has come,' he replied, 'and your father has killed the fattened calf because he has him back safe and sound.'

"The older brother became angry and refused to go in. So his father went out and pleaded with him. But he answered his father, 'Look! All these years I've been slaving for you and never disobeyed your orders. Yet you never gave me even a young goat so I could celebrate with my friends. But when this son of yours who has squandered your property with prostitutes comes home, you kill the fattened calf for him!'

"'My son,' the father said, 'you are always with me, and everything I have is yours. But we had to celebrate and be glad, because this brother of yours was dead and is alive again; he was lost and is found.'" (Luke 15:25–32)

The older brother was ticked off. He wanted no part of this party. It appeared that Dad had lost another son. Again, it was the father who did the seeking and went out to him. He encouraged his disgruntled heir to join the festivities. It would certainly dampen the joyous mood to have the older brother refusing to attend the celebration.

In reply, the oldest son made clear his complaints. "How could you? I've slaved for you. I have been your servant, always at your beck and call. I have been the good son, submissive, obedient, and faithful. For all of my compliance to your orders, you have never rewarded me with a party. But your son has wasted it all with whores and still you celebrate."

Those angry words are telling. He called the prodigal "your son," not "my brother." He also slipped in an accusation as to how the boy wasted the money. Remember, there is no indication of that in the story itself. The older brother had no way of knowing how the boy had spent the inheritance. He was so far out of the loop that he hadn't even known the boy was back. So this characterization of squandering the money on prostitutes was a charge without evidence to try to make this party hosted by the father seem ridiculous. By those words, Jesus showed that the stay-at-home son was just as far away as the prodigal had been. This respectable son was lost in his father's house. "Religious older brothers often miss the Father's joy now and forever. What a tragedy!"[13]

The father was still gentle in his reply. He explained, "We had to celebrate. It was a necessity. We had no choice but to party, because your brother has been found." Notice again the switch. Not "my son," but "your brother." To those religious grumblers who were critical of the riffraff gathered around Him, Jesus made clear that God celebrates over every repentant sinner found.

Kate Amerlan is a lovely young woman from our church who is serving the Lord in Athens, Greece. My wife Amy and I were part of a small team who went on a work trek to Athens to support Kate. There are a number of ministries Kate is involved in. Most deal with refugees, but one significant outreach is to prostitutes. In a section of the city that is filled with brothels and streetwalkers, Kate's mission team carries out a ministry called "Lost Coin."

My wife and I had the privilege of participating one night. Amy was part of a team of three women who went from brothel to brothel carrying a basket of treats and literature. Another man and I trailed along behind, waiting, watching, and praying. It was difficult to stay at a distance as the three women would disappear into a seedy hotel. At each stop, the women would talk to the owner of the brothel and any of the prostitutes that they could. The object was to show the love of Jesus, begin to establish a relationship, to offer them literature, and ultimately to invite them to an afternoon Bible study.

Among the female prostitutes were a number of transvestites and transsexuals. Takis was one of the transvestites who was willing to speak to the women that night. Amy was filled with compassion for this man. He seemed overwhelmed with sadness and despair. He sat outside the brothel wearing a dress, wig, and makeup and exuding despondency. The wig didn't fit, and the dress did nothing to mute the bulky, manly shape underneath. His bright red lipstick covered well beyond the outline of his lips. This wide swath of red around his mouth created the image of a sad clown.

As the women assured him of God's love and care for him, Takis expressed his hopelessness. He knew the answers, he knew the way out, but he was not ready or maybe just unwilling to respond. Knowing that God would forgive him seemed too good to be true. Takis appeared close to "coming to his senses," but not yet.

The women moved on to minister to others in similar circumstances. But Takis remained, lost on a dark street, having removed himself far from a loving Father.

The message of these lost things is for Takis and for all of us. It is God who is doing the seeking after each of us. He is far more interested in finding us than we are in finding Him. "In the work of redemption on the cross Jesus revealed the seeking grace of God to the utmost."[14] In the sacrificial death of His one and only Son, God the Father has made it possible for lost humanity to be transformed into His holy sons and daughters. That is why Jesus came to this earth.

Luke himself recorded the words of Jesus. "For the Son of Man came to seek and to save what was lost" (Luke 19:10). Christianity is the story of how God seeks after us. The Father passionately cares about His lost ones and is ready to give us a welcome that we do not deserve. Since that is true, what must we learn from this parable?

GOD CELEBRATES OVER EVERY REPENTANT SINNER FOUND: SO NEVER GIVE UP

The great focus of prayer for the church and the greatest cause of celebration for all followers of Christ should be for the prodigals among us. So many of us have a prodigal in our family. As a pastor, I have become aware of many of those in my own congregation. There is even a group of women in our church who banded together years ago to pray for wayward sons and daughters. I don't know how many of them have yet seen any answer to their prayers, but I encourage them never to give up.

After preaching on this familiar chapter, I was made aware of a number of others in the same situation. Several people phoned, wrote notes, or had a personal conversation with me about their own prodigal. The pain and longing is real and acute. For some, it is over a son who once professed Christ, but now seems to have rejected Him. For others, it is a daughter who never made any commitment to follow Christ and seems to get farther away with each passing year.

To every individual or family who is heartbroken over the waywardness of a loved one, I say, don't give up on him or her. Be as constantly concerned as the shepherd was for the lost sheep; be as diligent in looking as the woman was for the lost coin; be as ready to welcome and rejoice as the father was for his son.

But the parable is not about our seeking; it is not about our desire for wayward ones. The parable is very definitely about God's pursuit of the lost ones. No matter how hopeless someone may seem, no matter how long he has been gone, no matter how far he has run, as long as there is life there is hope. "Sadly, it is often not until we reach the pigpen that we come to understand the glory of the Father's house."[15] It may be in desperation, during the very darkest circumstances, that the lost ones will come to their senses. The Father is still seeking, so never give up on anyone.

GOD CELEBRATES OVER EVERY REPENTANT SINNER FOUND: SO SHARE HIS JOY

Instead of being concerned about what is fair, we should learn to party over the things that make God happy. The welcome and forgiveness of God have nothing to do with fairness. If they did, none of us would qualify. How easily we make self-righteous judgments of others. We size people up based upon our own criteria of respectability, our own agenda of righteousness.

That is no more nor less than what the Pharisees and religious teachers were doing as they sniffed contemptuously at those surrounding Jesus. We can fall into the trap of rejecting those Christ has drawn to Himself. We can become arbiters of those we believe worth being chosen by God for His very own.

I have encountered Christians who express feelings of hatred for a particularly depraved personality. I remember one person who simply loathed a popular comedienne and actress. Yet we have no right to dictate which people qualify to receive God's forgiveness. The Bible says that no one is righteous. No, not even one. All of us apart from the cleansing power of Christ are depraved prodigals. None of us deserves the welcoming forgiveness He offers. If we criticize God's grace, we can't share God's joy. If we don't care about and long for the return of the wayward and the rebellious, then we are like the Pharisees and teachers of the Law who criticized Jesus. Unless we celebrate and share the Father's joy when sinners repent, we are the self-righteous older brother lost in his father's house.

"The main point of the parable—that God gladly receives repentant sinners—must not be obscured."[16] We must take care that we do not join the ranks of the unforgiving, the ones who feel they are "slaving." The uptight, self-righteous religious people actually are less a part of the family than the wayward child who returns. They may seem to have less baggage than the one who has had a wild time, but inwardly they can be much farther from God than the repentant one. So we must be sure that we rejoice with God over the things that make Him happy. The return of a wanderer is one of those things. This should be the joy of our hearts, the passion of our prayers, the focus of our energies. Share His joy.

GOD CELEBRATES OVER EVERY REPENTANT SINNER FOUND: SO COME BACK HOME

You may be far from God as you read these words. It might not even seem that way to those around you. Your body may be present at church, but your heart is not there. Your mouth may speak the right words, but your mind screams something very different. You may be angry with God over something. You may relate to the feelings of the older brother, and you might share similar complaints. "God, I've slaved for you. Here I've been an obedient lackey, trying to do the 'right' thing, and this is what I get. You haven't rewarded me for being faithful, and yet look what you've done for him or her."

You may be far away from God in your behavior. You may be spending your lusts and passions on all the wrong things. You may be investing your money and time in all the wrong places. To all who are in such distant countries, the message is one of hope and relief. It is not too late to come back. The Father is seeking you. He has gone out into the night looking. He has searched the house, turned it upside down in the desire to find what was lost. He is standing outside the village every day, peering down the dusty road, waiting for you. He longs for you, not for excuses or promises to do better or bargains to be made. His arms are open, and His heart is full of love for you. So come back home.

* * *

George felt completely helpless. Ever since Sylvia died of ovarian cancer, leaving him with five children to raise, George had struggled. He had done the best he could, but handling five preteens was a challenge for any two parents, let alone one solitary dad. Each child was unique, handling the mother's death and the challenge of growing up in different ways and with varying degrees of success.

Nicole, the oldest daughter, had been the easiest. She immediately became the mother of the family, helping with cooking, cleaning, and even discipline. She had shown maturity beyond her years and now had a family of her own to care for. Cynthia and Edgar had some rough years through high school, but now seemed settled and secure. George was confident that their experiments with alcohol and rebellion had been just that—experiments. Now both were doing extremely well in college. Tina, the youngest, had been too little to even remember her mother. She was the model child now, struggling with all the things every young teen faces but growing up just fine.

Then there was Ben. The middle son had been the major source of George's trials and white hair. Ben was just old enough to remember Sylvia and just young enough to never properly deal with his bitterness and resentment over losing her. He acted out his frustrations at school in fights, disrespect to teachers, and truancy. Big for his age, the dark-haired boy used his height and weight to his advantage. Again and again, George had to take time off from work to meet with concerned teachers, principals, and counselors. He worked hard to keep his son in school, knowing that if he lost that opportunity, Ben would only go into a tighter downward spiral.

When things started to disappear around the house, George at first denied it. His wallet always seemed to contain ten or twenty dollars less than George thought he had. Tina complained about the loss of money from her piggybank. Finally, enough items came up missing that George knew Ben had to be stealing from his own family.

George searched his son's room, finding none of the missing items, but he did discover a small bag of white powder. From that moment on, George knew that the problem was beyond him and immediately got Ben into counseling. In the sessions, Ben would alternate between repentance and belligerence. Every time George thought they were making progress, Ben would make some gigantic leap backward. George had never felt so helpless before, but the worst was yet to come.

While at work, George received an emergency call from the school. Ben had threatened another student with a knife, and the police were involved. Late that night George finally arrived home, exhausted, with Ben in tow. The young man was suspended for the rest of the school year, and George had no idea what to do next. The two of them argued, and the frustrated father struggled to control himself, but angry words flew back and forth as if they were lobbing grenades.

Suddenly, a second too late, George saw his son swing at him. When he came to consciousness, he was crumpled amidst shards of glass from the bottle that had smashed into his temple. He tasted blood in his mouth and saw a puddle of it around him. With shaking hands he dragged himself to his feet and soon discovered that Ben was gone. The boy had taken some of his clothes, all of George's cash, and disappeared.

The phone call George was dreading finally came. The police had picked Ben up in a crack house downtown. The bedraggled figure George saw in the cell did not look like his son. Filthy, tattered clothes hung from his scrawny frame. Angry red marks dotted his arms. The eyes were empty, even of hate. The smells were overpowering.

Once George got him home and cleaned up, Ben slept for twenty-four hours straight. When he finally awoke, the boy was tearfully contrite, clearly in anguish over what he had done, pleading for another chance. George gladly gave it to him. Over the next two weeks, sleep and good meals transformed the wayward boy into a happy son. George was thrilled.

One day, when George returned from work, the young man was gone. This time he had taken anything he could. The televisions, VCR, camera, microwave, almost everything of value. But it was when George noticed Sylvia's dresser drawers open that he became sick. Ben had taken every piece of his mother's jewelry. A pearl necklace, a brooch that had been passed down from her grand-mother, gold chains, and worst of all, her wedding rings. Distraught beyond words, George began the hunt for his son. He scoured the streets, visited the shelters, explored dangerous neighborhoods hoping to spot a crack house that he could search, and he called the police daily, all without success.

Eight months after this second disappearance, George was jolted from a sound sleep by the phone. When he answered, there was no immediate response, but George knew better than to hang up. Within seconds there was a loud burst of liquid coughing, and then a husky whisper.

"It's Ben," the voice wheezed. There was the sound of crying, followed by more coughing.

"Daddy," he was sobbing now. "I'm sorry. I want to come home."

"Where are you . . . son?" George wondered if the word sounded as strange to Ben as it did to him.

"I'm a long ways away. I don't have anything. I can't afford a ticket. But I want to come . . . if you'll let me."

George wiped the tears from his own face.

"Yes, son, I want you home."

"Dad . . . Pop. I sold it all. There's nothing left. Mom's stuff, her rings, they're gone." The voice trailed off into uncontrolled weeping.

"I know, son. It's OK. Come home. Come home now. Don't wait another night." It was six in the morning when Ben trudged off the plane and toward the gate. He had hit absolute bottom over the past few months. He was an addict, inflicted with a venereal disease and per-haps worse. His emaciated body was covered with cast-off clothes. A dirty jacket did little to ward off the windy winter air. He knew that he smelled as bad as he looked, for the people seated near him on the plane had asked to be moved. Now he was finally back home. Was it possible?

Sure, his father had purchased this ticket for him, but Ben wondered how he would be received. How could Dad forgive him for all that he'd done? But he had to try. There was nowhere else to turn. Ben entered the terminal, his red, watery eyes scanning faces for sign of his father. The sound of cheers made him turn to his left. The first thing he saw was a big, handmade sign. In bold red letters it said, "Welcome back, Ben. We love you."

Holding the sign was George, and standing next to him were Nicole, Cynthia, Edgar, and Tina. George dropped the sign and opened his arms. Ben raced to his father. George's arms encircled him, drawing him close. Through his dirty, matted hair, he could hear his father whisper, "Welcome home, son."

* * *

Jesus wants us to know that such is the Father's love for us. His arms are open in welcome, ready to rejoice over our return. With this understanding and perspective Jesus presents of God, there are some responses we should determine to cultivate.

- I will learn to celebrate the things that delight God Himself.
- I will keep on praying for the prodigals around me, even those whom others view as a "lost cause."
- I will make every effort to rejoice over repentant rebels, because God's arms are open for their return.

• I will not hesitate to come back to my heavenly Father, because I know He longs for my return above all else.

God celebrates over every repentant sinner found, so never give up, share His joy, come back home, and join the party.

Notes

1. Douglas Beyer, *Parables for Christian Living* (Valley Forge: Judson, 1985), 49.
2. William Hendriksen, *Exposition of the Gospel According to Luke*, New Testament Commentary (Grand Rapids: Baker, 1978), 745.
3. H. A. Ironside, *Addresses on the Gospel of Luke* (New York: Loizeaux, 1955), 488–89.
4. David Wenham, *The Parables of Jesus* (Downers Grove, Ill.: InterVarsity, 1989), 101.
5. Ibid., 105.
6. Hendriksen, *Exposition of the Gospel According to Luke*, 749.
7. Ibid., 753.
8. Norval Geldenhuys, *Commentary on the Gospel of Luke*, The New International Commentary on the New Testament, ed. F. F. Bruce (1951; reprint, Grand Rapids: Eerdmans, 1979), 411.
9. Ibid., 407.
10. Kenneth E. Bailey, "The Pursuing Father," *Christianity Today*, 26 October 1998, 38.
11. Ibid., 39.
12. Beyer, *Parables for Christian Living*, 65.
13. Lloyd John Ogilvie, *Autobiography of God* (Glendale, Calif.: Regal, 1979), 26.
14. Geldenhuys, *Commentary on the Gospel of Luke*, 402.
15. Gary Inrig, *The Parables* (Grand Rapids: Discovery House, 1991), 18.
16. Walter Liefeld, in *The Expositor's Bible Commentary*, ed. Frank E. Gaebelein, D. A. Carson, Walter W. Wessel, and Walter L. Liefield (Grand Rapids: Zondervan, 1984), 8:983.

chapter seven

Taming
of the
Shrewd

"The Shrewd Manager"
Luke 16:1–15

Here's a Sunday school song you're not likely to hear, because the theme does not at all sound like it should be a spiritual virtue. It can be sung to the tune "Jesus Wants Me for a Sunbeam." It goes like this. *"Jesus wants me to be clever, as shrewd as I can be; crafty and cunning He calls me, astute let that be me. A shrewd girl, a shrewd boy, I will be shrewd for His joy. A shrewd girl, a shrewd boy, I'll be a shrewd one for Him."* As odd as that little verse sounds, it probably comes very close to expressing a real spiritual truth accurately. Believe it or not, being shrewd is a quality Jesus commended more than once. Just notice these familiar stories or sayings where Jesus used the very word we translate as "shrewd." The wise man who built his house on a rock was actually the shrewd man, according to Jesus (Matthew 7:24). The shrewd man with the rock-solid foundation in his life was contrasted with the foolish man who built his house on the sand.

Shrewd was what Jesus encouraged His disciples to

be as He told them to be as "shrewd as snakes" (Matthew 10:16; "wise as serpents," KJV). He coupled this charge with the quality of being as "innocent as doves" ("harmless as doves," KJV).

The wise virgins who brought extra oil for their lamps as they waited an extended time for the bridegroom were called shrewd (Matthew 25:1–13). These shrewd women had foreseen the possibility that the wait might be prolonged into the dark night, and so they prepared sufficiently. Jesus drew a sharp contrast between these women and the foolish virgins who had not anticipated a delay. So when Jesus told the parable of the dishonest manager and highlighted his shrewdness, it was an example for His followers of being shrewd for the kingdom.

Now shrewdness with money is not one of my strengths. I am not a financial wizard. I know next to nothing about stocks and investments. When I first came to the church I now pastor, one of the financial geniuses in our congregation was assigned to sit down with me and give me advice. I had no Social Security, no retirement plan, and I needed a great deal of help. Bob was doing his best to help me prepare for the future. He did everything but give me money. Yet in order to communicate with me in my financially impaired state, Bob basically had to use flash cards and talk really, really slow. About the only thing I remember from our little discussion was that you must be a long-term investor to be successful. If you are willing to put money in and leave it in whatever investment vehicle you choose, you should be all right in twenty-five or thirty years. In this parable about the shrewd manager, Jesus emphasized an even longer-term investment.

Jesus told his disciples: "There was a rich man whose manager was accused of wasting his possessions. So he called him in and asked him, 'What is this I hear about you? Give an account of your management, because you cannot be manager any longer.'

"The manager said to himself, 'What shall I do now? My master is taking away my job. I'm not strong enough to dig, and I'm ashamed to beg—I know what I'll do so that, when I lose my job here, people will welcome me into their houses.'

"So he called in each one of his master's debtors. He asked the first, 'How much do you owe my master?'

"'Eight hundred gallons of olive oil,' he replied.

"The manager told him, 'Take your bill, sit down quickly, and make it four hundred.'

"Then he asked the second, 'And how much do you owe?'

"'A thousand bushels of wheat,' he replied.

"He told him, 'Take your bill and make it eight hundred.'" (Luke 16:1–7)

This manager was an employee who cared for the funds or property of another. He had great authority to do business for his master, to negotiate, and even to sign contracts. "His was a powerful and responsible position, and a lucrative one."[1] It was from this position of trust and great responsibility that the manager was performing poorly, perhaps dishonestly. The accusation against him was that he was "wasting" his master's possessions.

Interestingly, Jesus used the same word *wasting* in the previous chapter. There it referred to how the Prodigal Son spent his inheritance money in a far country. There, as here, it meant to squander, to throw up into the air. There was no indication of exactly how it was spent, no moral judgment on what the money was used for—just that it was extravagantly tossed away. It seems, then, that the manager was guilty of mismanagement but probably not embezzlement. He was not known as the dishonest manager until he pulled another little trick that comes up later in the parable. But his failures did not go undetected. Word got back to the master, and he was called in for an open look at the books and ended up being fired. The manager was guilty and so didn't even attempt to defend himself.

The problem was that he didn't have any other career options. He was incapable of physical labor. Digging ditches was an impossibility for him, not because the work was beneath him, but because he did not have the strength, mobility, or health to wield a shovel. Neither would this manager resort to begging. He did have some moral standard, and asking for handouts was not something in which he was willing to engage himself.

Suddenly he had an idea. "I will make some friends now, who will take me in later." His plan involved those who owed the master money. They were most likely renters, tenants on the master's property. They owed a great deal to the master, which was probably back rent. Certainly, the manager has lost his position, but it obviously was not effective immediately. He had not yet been forced to clean out his desk, return his key to the executive washroom, and be escorted from the premises.

He had retained some powers for a short period of time, and so he needed to act quickly to carry out his scheme. He went to each debtor and had that debtor rewrite his note for a lesser amount. "This was clearly a scheme to make these renters personally indebted to him, and to achieve his purpose in such a manner that they would not complain or refuse hospitality to him after he has lost his position as manager."[2]

These were significant amounts of money that were owed, and each was reduced a significant amount as well. It was never the manager's intention to hide this from his master; such a feat would have been impossible. It would only be a matter of time before the master found out.

When the crooked dealing was discovered, the master's reaction was very interesting. The master commended the dishonest manager because he had acted shrewdly. "For the people of this world are more shrewd in dealing with their own kind than are the people of the light" (Luke 16:8). How the master responded may seem a little puzzling until you realize that he was stuck. The renters were undoubtedly overjoyed at that very moment. They were already praising the manager and the master to the heavens. Perhaps the master had even found out about the whole plot when the renters sent gifts, thank-you notes, and expressions of gratitude. How could the master possibly go to each of these debtors and say, "Sorry. My manager got it all wrong. You still owe me the full amount. Pay up quickly." Such an about-face would ruin his reputation.

Understanding the predicament that he was in and why his former employee had done what he'd done, the master commended, praised him. That what the former manager had done was deceitful was without question. The master himself characterized the man's actions as dishonest. But the man was shrewd, and the master had an appreciation for that. He basically called him a clever crook.

Shrewdness is to be discerning or sharp in practical matters. "The word 'shrewd' means keen, artful, astute and innovative."[3] The master applauded, not the dishonesty, but the cleverness displayed.

Some writers have real trouble with this parable. A

few have even suggested that Jesus was joking—that somehow Jesus was engaging in a bit of whimsy and jocularity. Surely, that is an unsatisfying and untenable reading of the parable. The lesson Jesus was communicating was clearly expressed. The main point Jesus made can be summarized in this sentence: *We must learn to use money for eternal investments.* There are three requirements for accomplishing this. Here is how we can be shrewd with a view to eternity.

BE GENEROUS FOR
THE GOOD OF OTHERS

My wife and I have always taken turns reading to our children before bed each night. Our oldest is now in high school and no longer needs such treatment, but our youngest is just now learning to read. Some books I enjoy reading to her. Others I dread. Some of the most dreaded ones are, unfortunately, Christian books. One series in particular elicits groans (silent, I hope) when produced for me to read. The books are long, often have an ill-conceived lesson, and have little to delight me as I read.

I used to spice up such books with my own invented plots and funny words, but this little one doesn't like alternate readings. Still, I read these particular books anyway because I hope that the spiritual point gets across.

One night after enduring one book from this series, I began to question our little one to see what she had learned. The story involved one character that was being terrorized by another. The first character decided to give a special gift to the bully to show his love and win over the threatening ruffian. The present was something very special and important to the little character. The thug accepted the gift and the two then became friends.

So I asked my daughter, "What is a good thing to do when someone is mean to you?"

She said, "Give them a special gift."

"That's a good idea," I replied. "And just what is a special gift?"

"A special gift is something you don't want anymore," she responded proudly.

All too often, those are the gifts that we are best at giving. Recycling wedding presents to our friends; giving castoff, useless items to the poor; or the infamous trick of sending used tea bags to missionaries. Yet, in telling this parable, Jesus was communicating that His followers are to be generous in a meaningful way.

There is some question as to where the parable stops and when Jesus begins speaking directly. The division is usually made in the middle of verse 8 or at the beginning of verse 9. But whether it is the master in the parable still talking or Jesus speaking directly matters little. Either way, it was Jesus who was articulating a truth, and those words are the obvious point of the parable He had just told. "I tell you, use worldly wealth to gain friends for yourselves, so that when it is gone, you will be welcomed into eternal dwellings" (Luke 16:9).

The forward planning and the discernment shown by the manager is characteristic of the forethought displayed by those who do business in the world. Business people show greater aptitude for such financial considerations than the people of God show for matters of eternal importance. This shrewd manager knew how to use money to bring future dividends. Jesus calls us to use money the same way. "Christians do not belong to this evil age, but they can nevertheless make responsible use of 'worldly wealth.'"[4]

How are we to go about doing such a thing? Is this

teaching us to secure a place in heaven by purchasing it? Of course not. As you can see from verse 1, Jesus was directing this parable at His disciples, those who are already following after Him. There is only one way to heaven and that is through faith in Jesus Christ. It is only by accepting the work that Christ has done for us on the Cross that we gain admission to heaven.

But a disciple had best use money to do something for the kingdom. It is vital that we be generous for the good of others. How we use our material goods should be governed by a pointed question: "Do we use our worldly possessions in such a manner that there will be persons in Eternity who will be glad to receive us?"[5] The ways in which we can or already do this are too numerous to mention. Let me use a few examples from those around me.

There are hungry people all around the world, but it is staggering to realize just how many are going without adequate food in urban America. In 1985, Ray and Julia Christensen began NewLife as a conduit to provide sustenance for people and children in the Chicagoland area. This mission has no paid employees.

Yet every other Friday for the past fifteen years, tons of food has been delivered to low income or no-income families. Single women, many of whom are grandmothers raising their grandchildren alone, head the majority of the homes. A portion of the delivery goes to underprivileged schoolchildren who are not fed adequately at home. All of the donated money goes to buy food at a food center for fourteen cents a pound. This charge simply covers the cost of processing, and the quality and variety of food available at that price is astounding. Volunteers rent a truck, load the food, drive into the city, and unload the food at the neighborhood church from which it is distributed. The deliveries average almost ten thousand pounds of food per month. Most of the people who are assisted by this ministry will never come in contact with the people who give and volunteer, at least not in this life.

The Kasalises are a family from Nairobi who got connected with our church about ten years ago. David, the father, was doing Ph.D. work at a nearby seminary. This African family was quickly adopted by many in the church. They stayed in our homes, were given furniture, and enjoyed hospitality, prayer support, and encouragement. When they returned to Nairobi, they went as members of our missionary staff. David is the president of the evangelical graduate school there.

About the time they were leaving, another African family came into our midst. They too were in the United States to complete degrees. They also became part of our church family, dearly loved and supported. Then the Wandawas returned to Kampala, and Philip Wandawa took up an administrative position in the school of theology, as part of our missionary staff.

Before the Wandawas had left, we were blessed with another African. Josiah Choms came to America to be seminary educated and to receive training as a pilot. In the four years he was here, Josiah completed a bachelor's degree and a master's degree, both with honors, and obtained a pilot's license and helicopter license. He is now in Nigeria, where he and his wife have begun a ministry to empower Africans to live productively. His ministry is modeled after John Perkins and his focus on the Three R's: Reconciliation, Relocation, and Redistribution.

When Josiah went back to his homeland, he too returned as a part of our missionary staff. Josiah is a soccer star in his own country. His dynamic testimony and passion for Christ will be greatly used to declare and demonstrate the gospel.

The point is that here are three families in whom many from our church have invested their lives. Now they are ministering on another continent. We seldom see them and will not likely see the results of their ministry with our own eyes. Still, we are convinced that we have invested our time and our money wisely.

The shrewd follower of Christ isn't so wrapped up in her stock portfolio that she cannot discover a way to give generously. Rather the shrewd disciple invests for the kingdom and has a kingdom perspective of possessions. "How can I maximize my money for eternity? This is the question of the shrewd disciple. We must be careful not to spend or give carelessly, sentimentally, or impulsively. The Lord calls us to be hard-nosed, clear-eyed, forward-looking, astute people."[6] The great concern for the disciple is not "How can I get my money working for me here?" Nor should my concern be "Can I retire at fifty-five? Can I afford this luxury car, or that exclusive membership?" The great objective for us as disciples is to see how we can invest our money for eternity. We must seek to give in such a way that people we have never met will welcome us in heavenly places.

What this means is that lives we never dreamed we had touched will embrace us. People we may have never met or even heard of will be there to greet us. When the day comes that we stand naked before God, stripped of all the things we value, will there be those there who can say, "It was your gift that brought the gospel to my village"? "It was you who brought food for my hungry children." "You gave so that I could go and preach." "You sacrificed, so that I could have the most basic necessities of life." We must use our money so that there will be people happy to see us in glory. Be generous for the good of others.

BE TRUSTWORTHY
WITH WHAT ISN'T YOURS

This is an obvious, yet significant and poignant point in this parable. The great preacher G. Campbell Morgan has an insightful little story that relates to this matter.

> Many years ago I remember in the home of a very wealthy man, who was a Church member and a Christian, one morning at Family Prayers he was eloquent and tender as he prayed for the salvation of the heathen, and for the missionaries. He was startled beyond measure when the prayer was over, one of his boys, a lad of ten, said to him, "Dad, I like to hear you pray for the missionaries." He answered, "I am glad you do, my boy." And the boy replied, "But do you know what I was thinking when you were praying, if I had your bank book, I would answer half your prayers![7]

Impertinent as the young boy may have been, what he said was telling and true. We often hold onto our money with a tight grip, all the while praying for God to use someone else to do what we ourselves could easily do. Notice the point that Jesus made next.

> "Whoever can be trusted with very little can also be trusted with much, and whoever is dishonest with very little will also be dishonest with much. So if you have not been trustworthy in handling worldly wealth, who will trust you with true riches? And if you have not been trustworthy with someone else's property, who will give you property of your own?" (Luke 16:10–12)

The manager made a future for himself with someone else's money. Talk about shrewd. He invested in his own future and didn't have to put any of his own resources on the line. That is exactly the perspective Jesus invites us to have as His followers. Whatever a disciple has belongs to the Master. If we claim to be the followers of Jesus, nothing we have is truly owned by us. At the end of the day, it all belongs to Him. Be faithful with it; use it for the Master and for His desires, because it is His anyway.

It was not any accident that Jesus referred to worldly wealth as "little." No matter how much money, how many acres of real estate property, or how many investment stocks you have, it is all little stuff. Worldly wealth is small potatoes.

How easily we fail to have that perspective. How quickly we put wealth and the wealthy upon a pedestal. How often do we not succeed in placing the proper value on earthly possessions. No matter what form money takes, it is all minuscule, simply the itty-bitty stuff, tiny in comparison to eternal riches. The point we must grasp is that if we aren't faithfully handling our comparatively petite possessions, our minute monies, how then can we be trusted with the truly big stuff? "If you have not been trustworthy in the use of material wealth, which, after all, is not really yours but belongs to Someone Else, namely, to God, then who will entrust to you the true, heavenly riches, your own possession, the kingdom prepared for you from the foundation of the world?"[8]

How we use what God has entrusted to us is a factor in our eternal blessing. This concept is not unique in the parables of Jesus. That our eternal *reward*, not our eternal destiny, is based on what we do now is a theme that runs through several of the parables. A disciple should be keenly interested in how his or her money is handled, for that is a significant factor in the reward to come. "What you will be given as your very own will depend on how you used the things of which you were only steward."[9]

Once we understand and remember that all of our possessions do not ultimately belong to us anyway, we should then move to use them in a manner that counts for eternity. "If anyone is unfaithful in connection with these 'borrowed goods' how can he expect to receive God's eternal riches, the spiritual gifts given for time and eternity to the redeemed as their own?"[10]

During the writing of this chapter, I had an experience that gave me a small inkling about how I might feel to stand before God and not have been trustworthy with what belongs to Him anyway. My wife and I were invited out for a special dinner by two couples from our church. We went downtown to a lovely restaurant. Following dinner, we were taken on a terrific tour of the city. The very knowledgeable and politically influential son of one of the couples conducted the tour. He drove the car in which the rest of us six rode as passengers.

As we neared the end of the excursion and a highly enjoyable evening, we had a minor accident. Our driver was cut off by one car and then sideswiped by another. The car that hit us then promptly drove off into the night. We all had had such a wonderful time that night that even this didn't dampen our evening. But then, it wasn't my car, nor was I the one driving. The son who was driving felt terrible. The car was a very nice one that belonged to one of the couples, not to him.

Yes, insurance would pay for it, and since we got the number of the car that hit us and ran, that would be covered too. Still, it is not a pleasant feeling to be using something that isn't yours and have it damaged while it is in your possession. If we could magnify that feeling a billion times, we might begin to imagine how we could feel someday standing before the Master of the Universe. The question is "Am I being faithful in using all that God has entrusted to me, in a way that brings Him honor?" This parable teaches us how to use forever what we have now. Remember, it's not yours.

BE DEVOTED TO GOD ABOVE ALL ELSE

Jesus talked so much about money precisely because it so easily becomes a greater object of our affection than God Himself. I remember the joke that involves a young man and his girlfriend. He says, "Honey, I've lost all my money. I haven't a penny to my name." She replies, "That's OK darling. It won't make any difference to me. I'll love you just as much—even if I never see you again."

Money can effortlessly become a primary factor in how we live and love. Too many times I have seen friendships destroyed over a profit margin. More often than I care to contemplate, I have seen marriages torn apart by the balance in a bank account. More frequently than you can imagine, I have seen members leave churches over matters of finance—because a stewardship campaign was proposed, or because the budget was increased, or because they heard a sermon that was forthright about the use of money. This is a subject that is too dear to our hearts.

Jesus closed this parable with a pointed statement regarding our relationship with money. "No servant can serve two masters. Either he will hate the one and love the other, or he will be devoted to the one and despise the other. You cannot serve both God and Money" (Luke

16:13). Jesus didn't infer that a disciple cannot have any money or that we must take a vow of poverty and live in total destitution. Rather, Jesus wanted His followers to understand that a disciple cannot serve both money and God. There isn't room in one life to have two supreme controlling influences. If you make the accumulation and enjoyment of earthly goods the focus of your life, you will fail with God. To love one will mean the eventual hatred of the other.

Jesus uses the word *devoted,* and it means to hold onto, or cling to something or someone. He contrasts that with the word *despise,* which means to think little or nothing of. So if you plan to cling to your possessions, eventually you will think little or nothing of God. And the same will be true if you reverse those desires. Whatever or whomever we serve becomes our focus. We become so obsessed with one thing that we give no significant time or thought to the other.

If you are going to be a shrewd disciple, you must be devoted to God more than to salary, revenue sharing, stock options, partnerships, savings accounts, property deeds, economic forecasts, or accruing interest. "Serving God can never be a part time job. Once a man chooses to serve God, every moment of his time and every atom of his energy belongs to God."[11]

The question Jesus would have us to ask ourselves is "Whom am I serving?" He wants us to evaluate the energy we spend each week, the time we invest each day, the thoughts we are lost in each hour and determine who our true master is. We can't have it both ways. Either we are clinging to God, or we have such a squeeze on our money that we can't hold onto anything else with security. Lloyd Ogilvie relates this story that gives us a hint of how to tell which master we may be serving.

A man confided in me an experience he had while going through his checks at income tax time. He's facing an excruciating divorce. He and his wife drifted away from the Lord and each other. His analysis of his checks over the past year unsettled him. He said, "I've just gone through what we spent last year. If I would have done that six months ago, I could have predicted the dilemma I'm in right now. So much money was spent on our own pleasure and luxury, and a pittance to the needs of others. Our self-indulgence has distorted our values. No wonder we lost our purpose and direction."[12]

As Jesus told the parable of the shrewd manager and gave His penetrating application, the Pharisees were listening in. Remember, Jesus was not directing this parable so much at them; rather He was telling it to His disciples. But this whole subject of money was in fact one of the weak points of the Pharisees. They did not appreciate what they heard and didn't like where the discussion was going. "The Pharisees, who loved money, heard all this and were sneering at Jesus. He said to them, 'You are the ones who justify yourselves in the eyes of men, but God knows your hearts. What is highly valued among men is detestable in God's sight'" (Luke 16:14–15). These religious leaders were caught up in their own importance, in loving money and what it could buy. In reaction to the parable, they turned their noses up at Jesus. They mocked His words and scorned the financial demands Jesus gave for the disciple.

You might feel that way right now. You might never admit it to anyone, but inside you just dismiss what Jesus has to say about the use of your money. It is tempting to sneer, to treat as unimportant and intrusive the teachings Jesus gave. But as shrewd as you are in business, as astute as you are in your career, as discerning as you are in the things of this life, so you and I must learn to use money for eternal investment.

In an insidious fashion, the love of money sneaks into our affections and distorts the values that we should have. It is like the raccoon that worms its way into the most tightly sealed garbage can. It infiltrates the heart as floodwater saturates a basement. It is something over which we should be concerned and vigilant. "If you are afraid that perhaps the love of money is getting a grip upon you just try giving away some of it, and if you feel more cheerful and happy than before, the love of money has not gotten hold of you. But if you find that it hurts to give, then you may well be fearful lest covetousness is getting a grip on your soul."[13]

Years ago I was part of a group of people who were trying to start a youth center for the community. There were numbers of troubled young people on our streets, and more were attracted to the city each day. In order to give these teens a place to meet, and someone with whom to talk, we established a place where they could gather. After a few years of great success, the facility we were renting became inadequate. The opportunity to purchase our own building, in a better location, became available. The only question was, could we raise the money to make it happen?

I remember talking with many people about this incredible opportunity for ministry. Some of the responses amazed me. Particularly I think about one businessman who said, "I don't have any kids here. My kids are grown now, and this center isn't in my community anyway." There was another couple who said, "We're retiring soon, and moving out of this area. We'll be gone and it doesn't seem like a good idea to invest in a ministry that we won't even be around to see in operation." I don't know whether or not these people were properly using their money in other ways. I don't have enough knowledge to condemn their lack of willingness to support that particular ministry idea. (By the way, the building was purchased, and last I knew the ministry was still going strong.) But I do disagree with the reasoning of those folks.

There may well be buildings we help pay for that will never be enjoyed by us. There will be missionaries we help train who may never come back to report to us, nor appear on our list of missionaries. There may be hungry people we help feed from whom we never hear.

There may be poor families we provide clothes for who will never send a thank-you. There may be financial needs in the church that we help to meet—and they are unglamorous needs like paying the utility bills or paying the custodian. There may be young people to whom we give a little money so that they can go to a Bible school or seminary, and yet they never come and minister in our church.

But if we are shrewd, we will use our money for things like those, for they are things that bring lasting value. Rather than funding extravagance for ourselves or for our children or grandchildren, we should invest for eternity. Instead of living in the lap of luxury, we should send our money on ahead by being generous, trustworthy servants devoted to God. I don't know how God wants you to use your money for eternal investments. He calls us all differently. But here are seven questions we should ask of ourselves, and ask them honestly.

- Do my expenses reflect generosity for the needs of others, or do they better reflect how I'm looking out for the comfort and pleasure of number one?

- Am I really using my money as if it belongs to God? Or am I using it as if it all belongs to me and my heirs?
- Which do I think about most often, with the greatest intensity and the deepest feeling: God or money?
- Can I begin to imagine that God has found me to be trustworthy with how I use "my" possessions?
- Is it possible that there will be people who welcome me in heaven because of how I have used my money on earth?
- Have I been faithful enough in the "little things" of finances to warrant being entrusted with the greater riches of God?
- Which gives a more accurate picture of my spiritual life—my Bible or my checkbook?

I opened my desk drawer today and there it was. A little blue toy car, just two inches long. It has flames painted on the hood and roof and the name "Flame Out" stenciled on it. The finish is all chipped and faded. The tiny wheels don't roll very well. That car has been with me a long time. It has moved from Massachusetts, to Toronto, to Chicago, from desk to desk to desk.

Let me tell you how it came to my possession. I was in my first pastorate, a charge for which I was painfully unprepared, underskilled, and overchallenged. I was probably five years too young to be a capable youth pastor and about fifteen years too young to be an effective pastor. Yet there I was, in my midtwenties, with all that responsibility and no ability. A church full of people (actually it was only about one-fourth full) with needs beyond anything I could handle. I was confident that nothing was too hard for God, but my fumbling attempts at being a pastor just kept getting in the way.

It was my birthday. I was turning twenty-five. One of the families in our church came to see me. At that time, my office was in our apartment. This family lived in those same apartments. The husband didn't come to church, but the wife and her daughter and son were there every week. They wished me a happy birthday. I was kind of embarrassed that anyone even knew it was my birthday. The little girl gave me a present she had made—a mobile of papers draped from a coat hanger.

And then it happened. Her little brother handed me his present. I still remember his face when he held out the gift. It was somber and serious, yet there was joy. In his small hand was this tiny blue car. It was his special car, a prized possession, his mother explained. I protested. This was too great a gift. He shouldn't part with this toy. But no, he wanted me to have it. His pastor deserved such a gift.

I must confess this all brought a lump to my throat. I treasure that car to this day. Oh, that God would give us the heart of a child to give in a way that brings God great joy.

Helmut Thielicke was right. "Our pocketbooks can have more to do with heaven, and also with hell, than our hymnbooks."[14] When the choice comes between our pleasures and extras and the needs of others, may we know what to choose. May we be willing to open our hands and give to the Lord what rightfully belongs to Him in the first place. And when God gives us the heart of a child and we use our money for eternal investments, then by God's grace there will be many to joyously welcome us into eternal dwellings.

Notes

1. David Wenham, *The Parables of Jesus* (Downers Grove, Ill.: Inter-Varsity, 1989), 162.

2. William Hendriksen, *Exposition of the Gospel According to Luke,* New Testament Commentary (Grand Rapids: Baker, 1978), 769.

3. Lloyd John Ogilvie, *Autobiography of God* (Glendale: Regal, 1979), 202.

4. Walter Liefeld, in *The Expositor's Bible Commentary,* ed. Frank E. Gaebelein, D. A. Carson, Walter W. Wessel, and Walter L. Liefield (Grand Rapids: Zondervan, 1984), 8:988.

5. Norval Geldenhuys, *Commentary on the Gospel of Luke,* The New International Commentary on the New Testament, ed. F. F. Bruce (1951; reprint, Grand Rapids: Eerdmans, 1979), 417.

6. Gary Inrig, *The Parables* (Grand Rapids: Discovery House, 1991), 116.

7. G. Campbell Morgan, *The Parables and Metaphors of Our Lord* (New York: Revell, 1943), 221–22.

8. Hendriksen, *Exposition of the Gospel According to Luke,* 772.

9. William Barclay, *The Daily Study Bible: The Gospel of Luke* (Philadelphia: Westminster, 1956), 217.

10. Geldenhuys, *Commentary on the Gospel of Luke,* 417.

11. Barclay, *The Daily Study Bible: The Gospel of Luke,* 218.

12. Ogilvie, *Autobiography of God,* 206.

13. H. A. Ironside, *Addresses on the Gospel of Luke* (New York: Loizeaux, 1955), 505.

14. Helmut Thielicke, *The Waiting Father,* trans. John Doberstein, (New York: Harper & Row, 1959), 103.

chapter eight

Tales from the Crypt

"The Rich Man and Lazarus"
Luke 16:19–31

Tom was a young man just out of college, ready to make his fortune in the world. His Uncle Morty had invited him to join his company in New York City. Uncle Morty had made a fortune in the stock market, and Tom was eager to learn from the best. The day he arrived, his uncle took him to lunch at an exclusive club. It was there, while waiting for their meals to arrive, that he promised to share his deepest financial secrets with his nephew. In fact, Uncle Morty confided that he had a stock tip to pass on that would eventually make Tom rich beyond his wildest dreams. Just before he could share the information, Uncle Morty became violently ill, right after the second bite of his swordfish special. The old man was rushed to the hospital, but within hours, he was dead from food poisoning.

Tom mourned for the loss of his uncle, but he was saddest over the fact that the man had been unable to share his secret to riches before he died. One night as Tom lay in bed, complaining and crying over his bad luck, he yelled out loud in desperation. "Uncle Morty, I beg you to come back and give me that tip so that I can have the life I've always dreamed of."

Suddenly his dead uncle appeared, right at the foot of Tom's bed. There was no mistaking the figure as the old man, and when he spoke, Tom had no doubt it was his uncle. "I've come to tell you what you need to hear," the hovering shape said. Tom was too ecstatic to be frightened. "Tell me, Uncle," he said breathlessly. "Give me your secret so that I may also have great success." Uncle Morty's spectral voice intoned, "Don't eat the fish." And then he vanished.

For all those looking for spectacular, supernatural information from the other side, it will do little good. Jesus told the story of such a man who believed that things would be different if he could just have a message sent from the dead to the living. Jesus made clear that this sort of communication was of no value. Instead, we must hear what God has to say *today* to those of us still in the land of the living. The lesson of this very unsettling parable was this: *Listen to God now, or regret it forever.*

Jesus introduced His listeners to an extremely wealthy man, an individual who was filthy rich. "There was a rich man who was dressed in purple and fine linen and lived in luxury every day" (Luke 16:19). The color purple itself was a sign of wealth. It was the color worn by royalty. The dye for the fabric was produced from a tiny purple shellfish or mussel and was very expensive to make. Fine linen was a delicate, soft, and costly fabric. When Jesus mentioned the man's daily life of luxury, the indication was that he feasted, enjoyed a banquet every day. This man was disgustingly extravagant, using every opportunity to show off his opulent lifestyle. "He made merry brilliantly; that is, he was living in dazzling, ostentatious splendor."[1]

"The description of the rich man's life presents two prominent features: the magnificence of his dress . . . next, the sumptuousness of his habitual style of living— a splendid banquet daily."[2] "The word used for feasting [was] the word that [was] used for a glutton and a gourmet feeding on exotic and costly dishes. He did this every day."[3] The problem was not the man's wealth but how he handled that wealth, how he flaunted it, and how he failed to put it to use to meet an obvious need.

Next Jesus introduced another man, but his situation is quite different. "At his gate was laid a beggar named Lazarus, covered with sores and longing to eat what fell from the rich man's table. Even the dogs came and licked his sores" (Luke 16:20–21). Every day, someone came and tossed the beggar at the rich man's front door. The word Jesus used indicates that he was dropped down without any specific concern for where he fell. They uncaringly dumped this poor man off right in front of the decorated front entrance of the rich man's home. This gate was another indication of the rich man's lifestyle. "Even when it is said that the beggar was laid at his gate, the word used is *pulon,* which means a gate full of artistry and exquisite beauty. He lived there in wealth and luxury."[4]

Notice the obvious contrasts between these two men. The poor beggar's body wasn't covered in gorgeous fabrics; it was covered with sores. He didn't feast every day; instead, he would have been overjoyed with table scraps. We should also notice that he was the only character Jesus ever named in one of His parables. The name *Lazarus* means "God helps." That was not incidental to the story. Rather, it was a very good indication as to why things turned out so differently for the two men. In the case of Lazarus, it was because God was his only help. This man was helpless, unable to care for himself. He couldn't even keep the scavenging dogs from licking his open sores. Some have represented this sore licking as a positive thing. It has been seen as beneficial to Lazarus because dogs tend to lick themselves when they are wounded to promote healing and because a dog lick generally is a sign of friendliness. However, I don't think that was the point of this detail in the parable. These were not house pets that surrounded the beggar; they were mangy street dogs. This was just one more indication of the helpless, wretched existence of the poor man. That these scavenging animals brushed their tongues over his ulcerated wounds was one final indignity over which he had no control.

Indeed, God was his only help. No one else even cared. Without stretching the information contained in the story, it is pretty safe to assume that the rich man couldn't avoid seeing this wretch. Since the beggar was at his front gate, the lavishly dressed property owner probably stepped over him on a frequent, if not daily, basis. Still, he paid no attention to the beggar. What opposite lives these two lived.

"The time came when the beggar died and the angels carried him to Abraham's side. The rich man also died and was buried" (Luke 16:22). Death comes to everyone. There is no amount of money that can chase away the inevitability of death. At the cessation of his earthly life, the misery of the beggar ended. He was not eternally tossed away by the uncaring; rather, he was escorted to his reward by angels. The angels took him directly to the side, or bosom, of Abraham. "Abraham was the great man of faith, the father of the faithful, God's friend. So the expression is a vivid way of saying that Lazarus is exalted to a position of the highest honor and intimacy in the heavenly fellowship of the saints. No greater reversal of fortunes can be imagined. Lazarus has been transported from the gutter to heaven's head table."[5]

This was certainly a position of honor, fellowship, and intimacy. "To the Jews that was a place of indescribable comfort and privilege."[6] The *side* or *bosom* is used in the Bible to describe the place of glory and communion which Jesus Christ enjoys with the Father. "No one has ever seen God, but God the One and Only, who is at the Father's side, has made him known" (John 1:18). This was the position John the Apostle enjoyed at the Last Supper. "One of them, the disciple whom Jesus loved, was reclining next to him" (John 13:23). The text literally reads that the disciple was leaning on Jesus' chest. There the disciple was in a place of friendship and familiarity. These are the implied blessings in which the poor man now delighted. "He who had yearned to receive crumbs and scraps is now reclining at heaven's table, where a banquet is being held."[7]

There was no mention of a funeral for the beggar. Likely his body was dragged out of the city and thrown on the mounds of burning rubbish outside the gates. This fiery trash heap was the place called *Gehenna,* which Jesus used as a picture of hell (see Mark 9:43). While Jesus made no mention of a burial for the poor man, he did say that the rich man was buried. It probably would have been the best funeral money could buy.

Just as the two men have been starkly contrasted to this point, so the differences continued after death. The wealthy man did not go to a place of comfort. He found himself in quite a different circumstance than the one that the beggar now enjoyed. "In hell, where he was in torment, he looked up and saw Abraham far away, with Lazarus by his side. So he called to him, 'Father Abraham, have pity on me and send Lazarus to dip the tip of his finger in water and cool my tongue, because I am in agony in this fire'" (Luke 16:23–24).

Many commentators warn that this parable was not given to provide a complete description of the life to come. While that is true, there are basic elements of the story that we should not hesitate to understand as Jesus' depiction of what happens after death. The rich man was in a place of conscious torture, misery, and pain. He was able to look up, literally lift his gaze and see Lazarus reclining in the place of comfort next to Abraham. Helmut Thielicke has made an interesting comment about the rich man's situation. "This is hell: to be forced to see the glory of God and have no access to it."[8] As presented here, hell certainly involves more than that, but perhaps of all agonies, this is the greatest: to be separated from God for eternity.

The rich man from his place of torment yelled out across the great distance to Abraham. "Send Lazarus here to relieve my suffering." Notice how the man still saw Lazarus as a subordinate, as inferior to himself, someone who was at his beck and call. His request for relief doesn't sound too helpful: a fingertip "baptized" in water, touched to his tongue.

Just a note here, that although I have believed and practiced baptism by immersion my entire ministry, I have always quibbled with the word. To *immerse* means to submerge something in liquid. It doesn't properly imply bringing it back up again. So rather than suggesting that I practice baptism in a way that brings death by drowning, I prefer the term *dip*. That is how the translators dealt with the word *bapsē* in verse 24. I practice baptism by dipping. This is a great relief to candidates to know that when I put them under the water, I have every intention of bringing them up again.

When I consider the rich man's request, it gives a real indication of just how agonizing it must have been. For him to simply desire a wet finger to touch his tongue allows us to glimpse the depths of his severe pain. We have met both men. We have an idea about their lives and see their condition after death. Now we discover more about the truth Jesus conveyed through the telling of the parable. In this story, we find three rea-. sons why we must hear and obey God's truth today. There are three reasons to listen to God now or regret it forever.

1. BECAUSE YOUR LIFE
SHOWS WHAT YOU BELIEVE

Over the previous year and a half, our church has had the privilege of ordaining four men for the gospel ministry. As part of the process, each candidate had to write a paper outlining his doctrinal beliefs, philosophy of ministry, and experience with Christ. Then the candidate faced an examining council. Each council member had the opportunity to grill that candidate with questions on virtually any relevant topic. Some council members grilled with a hotter flame than did others. The questions ranged from various early Christological heresies (false beliefs about Christ) to the candidate's personal habits, temptations, and weaknesses.

Although I have been involved in many ordinations, all of these were delightful for one reason. All four candidates were well known by our congregation. All four had ministered extensively to our people. All four had been involved in the church for a period, not of weeks or months, but of many years. When we officially recognized these men as gifted and called to minister the gospel of Jesus Christ, there was no concern that they were closet heretics. There was no hint of speculation that these were men who were unfaithful to their wives or abused their children. There was no underlying suspicion that these men were in the ministry for their own selfish motives or that they were looking for a way to financially profit from the ministry.

How could we have this confidence? It was because we did not "lay hands on," i.e., ordain, any of these men suddenly. It was after years of experience of seeing these four people live their lives in our midst. We watched them give themselves to ministry. We witnessed how they treated their wives and family members. We observed how their daily lives stacked up against what they were teaching and claiming to believe.

One of those candidates was Ray Christensen. I mentioned Ray in the last chapter in connection with a ministry he and his wife started. This man had been doing ministry for decades. He did not have extensive theological training. Yet now that he was pastoring a church in a nearby retirement center, he needed to be ordained. Both the council and the ordination service were filled with testimony of how God had used this man. Ray is not only someone who strongly believes in and deeply loves God but also a man whose life is a radiant testimony to that fact.

In response to the request of the rich man to receive some minute comfort from the hand of Lazarus, Abraham had a significant answer. "But Abraham replied, 'Son, remember that in your lifetime you received your good things, while Lazarus received bad things, but now he is comforted here and you are in agony'" (Luke 16:25).

The rich man wasn't in hell because of his money. Lazarus wasn't in heaven because he was poor. The rich man chose to receive all his good things in life only. He did not live out any faith in God during his time on earth. He didn't use his possessions for the good of others. Now Lazarus enjoyed blessing because God was his help, and the rich man suffered because he lived only for himself. "What we believe, and what we do about what we believe, determines our destiny."[9]

There is only one way to be saved, and that is through faith in Christ alone. But faith without works is dead. We can say we believe all we want, and we can even "ask Jesus into our heart," to use the popular phraseology. But if our faith is real, it will be seen in how we handle money and how we treat the Lazaruses in our lives. "We always live up to our beliefs—or down to them as the case may be. Nothing else is possible. It is the nature of belief."[10]

A church lay leader who is discovered in a pattern of adultery cannot excuse it all away by saying that he still believes but just has this little problem. What you really believe is shown by your life. This man believed that every woman he worked with was someone to be pursued and enjoyed sexually.

To carry the idea to a place where most of us live, consider this: whatever you allow to keep you from worship is a statement of belief. The schedule conflicts can be wholesome activities for your children, an extra morning of sleep to keep you functioning, or additional time on the job just to catch up. Whatever it is, that detour from worship says what you really believe. Your doctrinal statement then reads this way: "My daughter's soccer game is more important than God." "My rest is more important than God." "My career advancement is more important than God." You may be an extremely missions-minded person. You could be involved on a missions committee, write to missionaries, do short-term mission trips, or give substantially to the spread of the gospel. But if you never, ever mention Christ to those close to you, then you don't actually believe the gospel is good news. What you believe is shown not in a doctrinal statement, but in your life.

All too often, there is little difference between those who claim to be followers and the rest of the world. This is not so much a behavior problem as it is a belief problem. You say that you believe? Then remember this: a follower of Christ uses money for the good of others, not to show off or live in opulent extravagance. A disciple notices the Lazarus at his door needing love and attention. "There is a tragic insensitivity which engulfs us when we divide belief from caring about people."[11]

The rich man's statement of belief was on display by his extravagant lifestyle and utter disregard for the needs right on his doorstep. We don't have to hear what he actually believed. We don't have to know what religion he espoused. What he actually believed was amply illustrated by his daily life. Listen to God now or regret it forever, because your life shows what you believe.

2. BECAUSE YOU CAN NEVER COME BACK

I have long remembered a cartoon I saw that still makes me smile when I picture it. There are two lizards out in the middle of the desert. They sit looking out over the sand and cacti, warming their blood in the blazing sun. The first lizard says, "I just can't escape this strange feeling." "What feeling is that?" the second lizard asks. "The feeling that in a past life, I was someone called Shirley MacLaine." This brings us to a second reason why we must listen to what God says now. Contrary to popular belief, there is no other opportunity. Look at Abraham's words as he continued to explain why he could not grant the rich man's request.

> "'And besides all this, between us and you a great chasm has been fixed, so that those who want to go from here to you cannot, nor can anyone cross over from there to us.'
>
> "He answered, 'Then I beg you, father [Abraham], send Lazarus to my father's house, for I have five brothers. Let him warn them, so that they will not also come to this place of torment.'
>
> "Abraham replied, 'They have Moses and the Prophets; let them listen to them.'" (Luke 16:26–29)

Reincarnation is one of the oldest religious beliefs in the world and has become widely accepted in our country, especially over the past few decades. Yet the Bible is clear that there is no such thing. The rich man wanted movement between the worlds, but it was impossible. An enormous, gaping opening was set between them. It could not be bridged. The Bible tells us that humans are appointed to die once, and after that the judgment (see Hebrews 9:27). "Once a person has died, his soul having been separated from his body, his condition, whether blessed or doomed, is fixed forever."[12] There are no second chances, reprieves, or reincarnations. As horrible as hell was, this rich man would not escape. The choice had been made.

When he understood that there was no hope for himself, the tortured man begged for the chance to warn his brothers. Anyone who has flippantly remarked that he won't mind going to hell because all his friends are there should consider this. The reality is that this man was so miserable he didn't even want company. But this request would not be answered either. Lazarus would not return to alert the five brothers. They had the Scriptures, and that was enough.

Some time ago I visited someone who had gone to our church years before. Near the end of our visit the woman expressed how thrilled she was over a book she had been reading. The book had brought her great comfort during her husband's life-threatening illness. When she stated that the book was much more comforting than her Bible, I became very interested. She said, "This book told me a lot more about death and gave me peace about issues the Bible never even addresses."

Well, this was a book I had to read. She was more than eager to let me borrow it. It was a best-selling volume full of a tragic mix of New Age spiritualism and near-death experiences. The woman was gathering comfort from the idea that death was a moving toward the light and moving into another realm of consciousness, regardless of what or whom you trusted. I composed a "critique" of the book with some appropriate passages of Scripture and some of my observations. I included this when I returned the volume and never heard from the woman again.

Actually, the Bible has an incredible amount of information about the life to come. Some is extremely scary, to be sure. Eternity is shown as a fixed, permanent condition. But for those who know Christ, it is a place of eternal joy.

> No eye has seen,
>   no ear has heard,
> no mind has conceived
>   what God has prepared for
>   those who love him.
>   —1 Corinthians 2:9

Not wanting to accept this concept of eternal destination and finality, people gravitate to an eternal cycle of life. Recently I came across a book designed to teach children about reincarnation. It presented every human being as a raindrop. The colorful book wanted children to know that we humans are all unique and individual. We form up in the skies and float down to the earth where suddenly we find we are not alone. We gather into pools, we soak the grass, we nourish the gardens, and we float the boats. Then when we have done our job, we evaporate up into the skies, where we start all over again.

This is blatantly contradictory to the picture presented to us in Scripture. When the believer dies, to be "absent from the body" is to be "present with the Lord" (2 Corinthians 5:8 KJV). For the unbeliever, death brings separation from God forever. The relationship one has with God at death is set forever. "It is implicit in the account that one's attitude to God and his word is confirmed in this life and that it cannot be altered in the next one."[13] The rich man lived with no thought for his eternal soul. When his time came, he tragically discovered all his chances were over. There was to be no movement between the worlds. There was no going back or coming to. Listen to God now or regret it forever, because you can never come back.

3. BECAUSE YOU HAVE
ALL THE EVIDENCE YOU NEED

Bill Maher is the host of the television show *Politically Incorrect.* In a recent program, Mr. Maher seemed to scoff at the idea of the reality of a God-inspired holy book, such as the Bible. The idea that there could be a written word from God seemed to be ludicrous to him.

Maher's argument was that anyone who could make a tree wouldn't waste time writing a book. While that might sound reasonable to some, the reality is that a Creator who desired to be known and understood by His creation chose to communicate to humankind objectively. To write off this communication of truth is a deadly mistake. The suffering rich man objected to Abraham's contention that his brothers had Moses and the Prophets to warn them.

> "'No, father Abraham,' he said, 'but if someone from the dead goes to them, they will repent.'
> "He said to him, 'If they do not listen to Moses and the Prophets, they will not be convinced even if someone rises from the dead.'" (Luke 16:30–31)

Here is the crux of the parable. To really get the attention of the five brothers, the rich man was convinced that they needed to be visited by a ghost. The tormented rich man was convinced that if his brothers could just have a paranormal message, some really nifty miracle, then they would believe. In effect he said, "The Scriptures just didn't do it for me, Abe, so send a supernatural sign."

This is the Ebeneezer Scrooge mentality. As much as I love Dickens' classic tale *A Christmas Carol,* it centers on three ghostly apparitions that turn old Scrooge around. The transformation is terrific, but it has to come via a supernatural revelation. The knowledge and experiences he previously encountered had all been rejected. This is what the rich man expected his brothers to need. The truth is that Scripture is sufficient, and if they didn't get that, nothing would persuade them. Not even a resurrection.

Consider how much revelation the rich man had at

his disposal with Moses and the Prophets. Look at the truths available that should have been sufficient to change his behavior prior to his death. "If there is a poor man among your brothers in any of the towns of the land that the Lord your God is giving you, do not be hardhearted or tightfisted toward your poor brother. Rather be openhanded and freely lend him whatever he needs" (Deuteronomy 15:7–8). Or here, in this passage, where God ridicules the superficial religious observances being offered to him:

> Is not this the kind of fasting I have chosen: . . . .
> Is it not to share your food with the hungry
>   and to provide the poor wanderer with shelter—
> when you see the naked, to clothe him,
>   and not to turn away from your own flesh and blood?
> —Isaiah 58:6–7

These passages are clear about how to treat the poor and needy, about the kind of life a godly man should live. The rich man obviously ignored these things, and if his brothers were doing the same, then nothing would convince them. "We have as much witness from heaven as we need."[14] It was not a lack of evidence that put this man in hell; it was a lack of willingness to believe.

Like the rich man in hell, we may have thought, *If only God would do something spectacular, if He would heal this person or miraculously bless that situation, then I would believe, or then So-and-so would be convinced.* But this written Word of God is all the evidence we need. "The man who refuses to heed the clear, definite instruction of the Holy Scriptures would never believe though one came to him asserting that he had been on the other side of the tomb and had returned to warn him to flee from the wrath to come."[15]

Isn't it an irony that such a thing did happen not long after Jesus told this story? A man bearing the very name of this beggar was raised from the dead. That Lazarus had been dead for several days, there was no question of his demise. After Jesus called him from the tomb, the response of many who witnessed the event was to believe; yet others were moved only to attempt to kill Lazarus—and Jesus too.

A short time later, when Jesus was put to death, this supposed victory for evil was dashed by His glorious resurrection. Still there were more who refused to believe and accept this victory over death than there were those who became followers of Jesus. Those who did not want to believe were not convinced by "mere" resurrections.

God has spoken to us in Jesus Christ, the Living Word. God has declared His glory in and through creation. God has revealed Himself in the written Word. And if this is ignored, then nothing will work. "It is the plain fact that if men possess the truth of God's word, and if, wherever they look, there is sorrow to be comforted, need to be supplied, pain to be relieved, and if it moves them to no feeling and to no action, nothing will change them."[16] Listen to God now or regret it forever, because you have all the evidence you need.

When I first began full-time ministry, it was as a youth pastor. The high school youth group was made up primarily of young women. Perhaps this was partly due to my single status at the time. Most of the young men were no trouble at all. The majority of them seemed to be sincere, eager to take part, and generally on the right spiritual road.

On the other hand, the girls had several among their number who gave me no end of grief. Two of them in particular appeared to be almost without hope, at least to me. They seemed to pay little or no attention to what I was teaching. They were consumed with elements of popular culture that would do nothing but drag them down. All sorts of other events took precedence over their attendance at any youth function. Their main response to whatever was going on consisted of giggling and rolling their eyes.

By contrast, one of the boys in the group was a model citizen. He was popular, extremely involved, and almost always in attendance. He was an unquestioned leader of the group. I held out high hopes for his future as a spiritual leader in the church. Sadly, that has not been the case so far. The last I knew, this man has little or no use for God. His life bears no reflection of what he once claimed to believe. All that promise seems a relic of the past. I would never write him off, for nothing is impossible with God, but things aren't very encouraging from a human perspective.

On the other hand, those two girls have grown into exemplary women. One of them has an incredible musical gift she has used for the Lord. She married a pastor and is serving God faithfully in the church. The other woman is still at the church I served as youth pastor. Years after my ministry there, I returned. She rushed up to me with a hug and introduced me to her husband and children. I couldn't believe it. She had turned into a beautiful woman of God. "I want to thank you," she said with conviction. "Thank me?" I replied. The only thing I could imagine that she could thank me for was that I didn't strangle her during her teen years. "I want to thank you for how God used you in my life."

Obviously, there were many more influences in the lives of these two women than the tiny part that I played. There were other youth pastors, pastors, and teachers, along with their parents, who got through to them. What amazed me was that all the time when I thought that boy was listening, he was actually paying no attention. And all the time when I was convinced those girls were not listening, they did hear what God was saying.

How should we respond to this parable? Here are some suggestions on how to live in light of Jesus' message.

- I must make certain that my life actually gives evidence of what I say I believe.
- I must be alert to the Lazarus who may be lying outside my door.
- I must make the most of my life for God now, rather than living for myself.
- I must treasure the revelation of God, listening carefully to Him.

The lesson we must learn from this parable is never to ignore an opportunity to hear from God. Do not neglect His message. The message may come from the pulpit on Sunday or from a Bible study during the week or from the book you are reading right at this moment. The important thing is that we must listen to God *now* or regret it forever.

Notes

1. William Hendriksen, *Exposition of the Gospel According to Luke,* New Testament Commentary (Grand Rapids: Baker, 1978), 788.
2. F. Godet, *A Commentary on the Gospel of St. Luke,* trans. M. D. Cusin (Edinburgh: T & T Clark), 2:176.
3. William Barclay, *The Daily Study Bible: The Gospel of Luke* (Philadelphia: Westminster, 1956), 221.
4. G. Campbell Morgan, *The Parables and Metaphors of Our Lord* (New York: Revell, 1943), 224.
5. Gary Inrig, *The Parables* (Grand Rapids: Discovery House, 1991), 127.

6. Douglas Beyer, *Parables for Christian Living* (Valley Forge, Pa.: Judson, 1985), 85.
7. Hendriksen, *Exposition of the Gospel According to Luke,* 784.
8. Helmut Thielicke, *The Waiting Father,* trans. John Doberstein (New York: Harper & Row, 1959), 48.
9. Lloyd John Ogilvie, *The Autobiography of God* (Glendale, Calif.: Regal, 1979), 316.
10. Dallas Willard, *The Divine Conspiracy* (San Francisco: Harper, 1998), 307.
11. Ogilvie, *Autobiography of God,* 317.
12. Hendriksen, *Exposition of the Gospel According to Luke,* 785.
13. Walter Liefeld, in *The Expositor's Bible Commentary,* ed. Frank E. Gaebelein, D. A. Carson, Walter W. Wessel, and Walter L. Liefield (Grand Rapids: Zondervan, 1984), 8:991.
14. Alexander MacLaren, *Expositions of Holy Scripture,* vol. 9, *St. Luke* (reprint, Grand Rapids: Baker, 1984), 107.
15. H. A. Ironside, *Addresses on the Gospel of Luke* (New York: Loizeaux, 1955), 516.
16. Barclay, *The Daily Study Bible: The Gospel of Luke,* 223.

chapter nine

Prayers
God
Hears

"The Pharisee and Tax Collector"
Luke 18:9–14

I came across some advertising about prayer the other day. The ad was directed at people who were looking for answers to their prayers and featured a picture of a bowl. With great curiosity, I read the posting. I soon discovered that the bowl was very central to the whole concept about prayer presented by the religious organization that sponsored the ad. Of course, this wasn't just any piece of pottery. This bit of crockery was the Crystal Prayer Bowl. Here is how it worked. All prayer requests that were sent to this particular Temple were collected in the bowl. The bowl-full of requests was then placed under the Blue-White Healing Light at the beginning of healing sessions in the Sanctuary. The claim was that in this way the requests received all the energy and petitions of those who attend the session.

The ad went on to encourage the reader to put into the bowl the name (or even the initials) of anyone or anything needing prayer or healing energy. The endorsement then stated that the whole process had proven to be very effective and that the bowl had an excellent rep-utation. Lest the petitioner think that his request would only receive one session in the bowl and then be thrown away, the ad promised a different ending. It seems that once the bowl was full, the requests were taken out and placed inside the walls of the "Upper Room," where they would continue to benefit from the powerful energy pro-duced by that location.

Is prayer some gimmick, or energy, a complicated ritual, or some form of incantation that brings remark-able success? No, prayer is quite simply defined as ask-ing God. Jesus said, "Ask and it will be given to you; . . . how much more will your Father in heaven give good gifts to those who ask him!" (Matthew 7:7–11). Prayer is making requests of the One who is greater than we. "The picture of prayer that emerges from the life and teach-ing of Jesus in the Gospels is quite clear. Basically it is one of asking, requesting things from God."[1]

The New Testament writer James pointed out our human tendency to try to do things on our own without God's help. He listed the extremes to which we are will-ing to go in our attempts to achieve what we want. Then James put his finger on the real problem. "You do not have, because you do not ask God" (James 4:2). Prayer is talking to God, making our requests known to Him. But not all of the things we refer to as prayer are heard by God. "Just talking to God is not prayer, though prayer is talking to God."[2] Not all words addressed to God qualify as prayer, no matter how cloaked they are in religious terminology. Not every request is worthy of God's care-ful attention, even if it is placed in a special bowl and ra-diated with a blue light.

Jesus told a story to keep us from praying ineffective prayers. The Messiah was concerned about those afflicted with religion and self-esteem. These can become the two major obstacles in accomplishing real prayer. Perhaps I should qualify those words this way. Jesus spoke against prayers that were infected with mere religion and excessive self-esteem. Mere religion is just superficial methodology. Excessive self-esteem is misguided gratitude. It is wrongly focused appreciation combined with delusions of grandeur.

Jesus pointed out these obstacles to prayer through this familiar story. In the parable, we have two different men, praying two different prayers, with two entirely different results. "To some who were confident of their own righteousness and looked down on everybody else, Jesus told this parable: 'Two men went up to the temple to pray, one a Pharisee and the other a tax collector'" (Luke 18:9–10). This parable had a very specific target. It was directed toward people who trusted in and believed in themselves at the same time they turned up their noses at everyone else. These people, who snubbed others while acclaiming themselves, were the target as Jesus aimed a pointed story from daily life in their direction and let the arrow fly.

The temple was the center of Jewish life. Every Jew experienced its significance. The temple was the place for public religious services, as well as the location many used for their personal communication with God. "The temple was used not only for public religious transactions, for the bringing of sacrifices, and for teaching, but also for private devotions."[3]

To better understand Jesus' point, we must realize who these men were that arrived to pray in the temple. When we hear the name *Pharisee* today, it generally has a bad connotation. These men always seem to be the bad guys in the stories we hear about Jesus in Sunday

school. No one wants to be considered a Pharisee in today's world. Even those who know nothing about the
Bible can be heard to bandy about this epithet for
hypocrisy and self-righteous behavior. We must remember that none of this was the accepted understanding in
the time of Jesus. "The Pharisee represented the pinnacle of Judaism. They were deeply religious laymen, committed to upright behavior and religious tradition. They
were highly respected by the general public as good
men. They cared deeply about spiritual matters."[4] The
people of Jesus' day considered the Pharisees to be on a
higher spiritual plane than they were, people who had
an undeniable "in" with God.

Actor Bill Murray did an interview years ago in which
he revealed that his sister was a nun. His happy take on
the situation was, "She's got us all covered." Murray
may have been joking, but his words represent a prevalent concept. The popular idea is that God will always
accept certain religious people. In fact, the reasoning
goes, if not them, then whom? If God doesn't pay more
attention to the cares and prayers of a nun, or pastor, or
missionary, or priest, then who has any chance at all of
being heard? So for the crowd to hear that the Pharisee
was going to pray a prayer that God did not hear would
be quite a shock.

Even more shocking was the person behind the
prayer that God did hear. Tax collectors as a group may
seem to take a beating in the gospel accounts. The profession is generally mentioned in a derogatory way. This
has been pointed out to me by the handful of government tax people I have had in my congregations over the
years.

In reality, stories of individual tax collectors com-
prise a couple of the most encouraging stories of re-

demption in the New Testament. Consider Matthew, the tax collector who left his booth to follow Jesus. He became one of the twelve disciples and wrote one of the Gospels. Matthew 10 records a list of the twelve, and it is interesting to note that Matthew is identified as "the tax collector." None of the other eleven on that list is connected with a profession. Simon the Zealot is identified by his former *political* association, but Matthew includes his *job title*. Knowing what we know about how tax collectors were viewed, there is only one explanation that makes much sense. Matthew was showing humility and demonstrating the depths of God's love and the magnificence of His transforming power. Even a tax collector can be saved.

The other famous tax collector is Zacchaeus. Luke 19 records the remarkable story. Here is a guy even worse than Matthew. Zacchaeus was a *chief* tax collector. It is clear that this man had cheated and swindled his way to wealth. His encounter with Jesus brought him to repentance. The transformation was enough to cause him to return fourfold all the money he had gypped from people.

These two transformations were observed with surprise by most people. Perhaps others even viewed them with suspicion, wondering what new angle these guys were trying now. The general perception was that tax collectors would always need redeeming, and most likely that they were even beyond any hope at all.

Tax collectors were not viewed as the honest, compassionate, stellar citizens they are today. "The tax collectors were as bad a lot in most people's eyes as the Pharisees were good."[5] The Roman government allowed them to keep whatever additional money they could extort from the people above and beyond the taxes. In the eyes of the crowd, if any person's prayer would not be heard by God, it would be the tax collector's.

Through these two very opposite individuals in the parable, Jesus showed believers how to pray so that God would hear them. The lesson of the parable can be expressed this way: *When we pray humbly, God pronounces us righteous.* First of all, note the characteristics of these two contrasting prayers and begin learning how to pray in humility.

THREE CHARACTERISTICS
OF SELF-RIGHTEOUS PRAYER

I love to fish. I don't get the opportunity to fish very often, and it is mostly confined to vacations. This is especially true because Illinois, specifically the area around where I live, is not noted as a great fishing location. After years of not fishing at all, I recently began to go more frequently, often with my daughters. This is something that we can enjoy or endure together, because things are a lot more pleasant if we actually catch fish. Most of all I fish for bass. I appreciate the challenge and fight of smallmouth and largemouth bass more than just about any other type.

On one of our fishing trips together, I hooked into a rather small fish. My younger daughter was right beside me jumping up and down with glee. This is actually something she does all the time, but right then it was because I was hauling in a fish. When I finally got the little tiger up to shore, I examined it carefully. For some reason, I couldn't tell whether it was a large rock bass, a small largemouth bass, or a small smallmouth bass. Each of those fish has distinct characteristics that aid in identification, but in this case, I was uncertain. So I said out loud, "I'm not sure what this is."

A man nearby took a look at what I was holding and contributed this thoughtful reply: "I think it's a fish." Of course he was right. If it swims like a fish, looks like a fish, and smells like a fish, it must be a fish. Jesus didn't come right out and call the Pharisee or his prayer self-righteous. But everything about the prayer characterized it as such. It looked, swam, and smelled of overconfident, egotistical presumption. "The Pharisee stood up and prayed about himself: 'God, I thank you that I am not like other men—robbers, evildoers, adulterers—or even like this tax collector. I fast twice a week and give a tenth of all I get'" (Luke 18:11–12). Consider each of these three characteristics, for they can guide us so that we might avoid self-righteous praying in our lives.

I Am Confident in Myself

Characteristics of audacity are apparent in the details Jesus gave about the Pharisee in His story. Even the idea of where he stood gave an indication of brazenness. When we read later on in verse 13 that in contrast to the Pharisee the other man stood at a distance, it implies that the Pharisee stood as close as possible to the holy place. It is likely that the Pharisee made an effort to be nearest to the location of greatest sanctity. It appears he had no compunction or reservations about being on what was in his mind the hallowed, sacred spot closest to God. (That he was standing at all is no sign of impudence. Standing is the common Jewish mode of prayer, as can be seen today at the Wailing Wall in Jerusalem.)

Additionally, if we focus on the language he used in his prayer, this man's confidence is evident. He used "I" with frequency. "Outwardly he address[ed] God, for he [said], 'O God.' But inwardly and actually the man [was] talking about himself to himself."[6] The Pharisee's entire prayer was an expression of boldness and confidence based upon his own goodness. "The Pharisee did not really go to pray; he went to inform God how good he was."[7]

Now there is nothing wrong with praying with confidence. In fact, Scripture enjoins us to do just that. "Let us then approach the throne of grace with confidence, so that we may receive mercy and find grace to help us in our time of need," says the author of the book of Hebrews (4:16). However, the boldness must not come from our own selves; it cannot be centered on our goodness and right to approach God. The biblical writer based the invitation to come boldly before God upon Someone outside of ourselves. In Hebrews 4:14 the author made clear that our confidence to approach God comes because "we have a great high priest who has gone through the heavens, Jesus the Son of God." Praying with confidence can only come when we are trusting in the goodness of Christ, rather than in ourselves. Being casual with God because we feel that we have it all together spiritually will result in a prayer that doesn't go beyond the ceiling. It is a waste of breath. The self-righteous Pharisee's prayer "never went higher than the inner roof of the temple court, and was, in a very fatal sense, 'to himself.'"[8] The confidence of the Pharisee was misplaced. His impropriety should be a huge orange detour sign, warning us to follow another direction in our prayers.

I Compare Myself to Others

This is the most obvious characteristic of the Pharisee's prayer, at least to us. The Pharisee was impressed with what he was like in comparison to others he had chosen to identify. He chose others who were outwardly worse than himself, and those others became the standard for his comparison. This was truly dangerous.

The other day I was reading a sports magazine I had just received in the mail. In it was a picture that caught my attention. The picture showed a huge man engaged in sumo wrestling with a man he dwarfed in size. The big guy was Emanuel Yarbrough, called the world's largest athlete. A former football player and then nightclub bouncer, this man is enormous. He is six feet, seven inches tall and weighs 728 pounds.

That's right, I had to read it twice myself: more than seven hundred pounds. The man he was wrestling in the picture was not really tiny at all. He was about my size, six feet, two inches, 250 pounds. While not exactly svelte, I felt pretty good while looking at Mr. Yarbrough. I was so impressed with the picture that I called my daughters over to check it out. The older one wrinkled up her nose and said, "Gross." The younger put her arm on my shoulder to console me and said, "You are _way_ bigger than him, Dad." A five hundred-pound weight difference had no meaning for her. She's certain that I'm the biggest guy in the world. This reminded me that comparisons with others are generally a very poor idea.

Unfortunately, not unlike the Pharisee, comparing is something in which we are apt to engage. "All of us are but too prone to regard ourselves as good and others as wicked."[9] It is not all that difficult to be impressed with what we are like in comparison to others. The problem is that such activity carries no weight (no pun intended) and is of no positive value. "Our status with God is not based on being better than others."[10] Whenever we engage in this game of comparing, our prayers become mere exercises in futility. They are more accurately mumblings without meaning, and recitations without result. Douglas Beyer gave an insightful list of some of the ways we can do comparison-shopping in our thought processes. His words revealed just how self-righteous we can sound.

> There are racial Pharisees who say, "Thank God, I am not like those lazy, shiftless blacks." And there are social Pharisees who say, "Thank God, I am not like those chiseling welfare freeloaders." And there are intellectual Pharisees who say, "Thank God, I'm not like those dull uneducated laborers." And there are charismatic Pharisees who say, "Thank God, I'm not like those spiritually dead Christians who don't speak in tongues." And there are even pagan Pharisees who say, "Thank God, I'm not like the sanctimonious Christians who attend church."[11]

Anytime we compare ourselves to others we end up being the losers.

I Congratulate Myself

Self-congratulation is no stranger to most of us. We pass along information that will help people to think better of us; otherwise, some of us would have nothing to say. When we meet someone, we have an urge to give this person a sense of who we are so that they can properly appreciate our importance. This tendency is part of human nature. It is something we have to fight against if we don't want to appear egotistical and self-absorbed.

The other day a stranger dropped by to see me. Although I had never met him, I had known members of his family when I was a little boy. For the twenty minutes that we were together, he caught me up on a large portion of the activities of his life—the accomplishments of himself and his wife, children, and grandchildren, even though I had no idea who any of them were.

He seemed to be saying, "You don't know me, but don't you wish you did? I have a very significant life."

Now that I think about it, maybe what annoyed me was that I never got to tell him how important I was. Such is the beguiling nature of self-adulation. This is characteristic in the prayer of the Pharisee. "Throughout his prayer the Pharisee is congratulating himself."[12] "It was less a prayer in which he gave thanks to God, than a congratulation which he addressed to himself."[13]

Haven't we all listened to our share of prayers that were nothing more than a bit of boasting about self? Haven't we heard a number of testimonies that were really just bragging about what the person accomplished? Even more embarrassing, have there been any such self-congratulatory prayers of which I myself am the perpetrator? Isn't it possible that even when we are alone with God we are tempted to pray with self-acclaim? We might say things along these lines: "God, I've worked in vacation Bible school all week, You must be so proud of me." "I've had devotions two days in a row; You owe me some blessing." "Isn't it terrific that I've given so much money to the church this year?"

The real crime in any self-congratulatory prayer is the theological statement it makes. "Notice this man was not thanking God for what grace had done for him; he was thanking God for what he himself had done."[14] That is what is wrong with such prayers. They are really an exercise in self-affirmation, rather than an expression of petition or adoration.

These three characteristics serve as sure signs of self-righteous supplications to which God pays no attention. We must guard against superficial religion and excess self-esteem, for these are landmines to true prayer.

THREE CHARACTERISTICS
OF HUMBLE PRAYER

The great evangelist Dwight Moody is reported to have said, "God sends no one away empty except those who are full of themselves." The Pharisee was full of himself and so went away empty. The tax collector presented not merely a contrast to the Pharisee, but the proper attitude and approach for prayer. "But the tax collector stood at a distance. He would not even look up to heaven, but beat his breast and said, 'God, have mercy on me, a sinner'" (Luke 18:13).

Jesus' words reflect three characteristics of humility in praying. These describe what our prayers must look like if we desire to be heard by God.

I Know God's Place

Notice that this man was reverent toward God. While still within the temple, he stood as far away from the holy place as possible. His prayer was to God, and in it he called upon God. It was not that the man didn't mention his own needs; he did that well enough. The important point is that the tax collector knew that God is the high, exalted One, enthroned in the heavens. "Only when God is truly seen for who He is can we see ourselves for who we are. Meaning comes only when life is theocentric, not egocentric."[15]

As popular as prayer is today, it is often seen as no more than a self-help tool. People believe and are taught that it does not so much matter to whom you pray, or how you pray; it all helps. But prayer that God hears is directed to Him alone. It is prayer recognizing that He is in charge, the Commander of the universe, the King of Kings and Lord of Lords.

Don't misunderstand me. Familiarity is not the problem. We can call Him "Daddy," Romans 8:15 tells us. Honesty isn't the problem. We can complain to Him and question Him. Such gripes and queries are what go on so often in the Psalms, in Job, and in the lives of some of the greatest servants of God. But in the midst of our familiarity and honesty, we must confess and declare that He is sovereign over all things. We must know that He is Jehovah, and there is no other besides Him. We must know God's place.

I Know My Place

The next characteristic displayed in the humble prayer of the tax collector was his understanding of who and what he himself was. This man was honest about his sin. He had a deep and real consciousness of the sin in his life. It sounds as if he had come in desperation to meet God. He was acutely and agonizingly aware that he had nothing to give and nothing of which to boast. This tax collector could only see his utter sinfulness and desperate need for forgiveness. Notice how the description of the man indicates his attitude of prayer.

- He was ashamed of his sins, and so he looked down.
- He was distraught over his disobedience and beat his chest.
- He hungered for forgiveness, and so cried out to God for mercy.

The Bible makes clear that our forgiveness and mercy only come through the death of Christ. This can only be appropriated when we agree that we are in dire need of God's provision in Jesus. It is all too human for us not to be able to accept that we are that needy, that sinful.

I recently read something written to encourage a teenager on how to have a fulfilling life. The piece stated that the teen needed to make a declaration of self-esteem in order to find fulfillment. The declaration involved admitting that everything about me belongs to me. I own it all, whether the all is my body, or my actions, or my feelings, or my aspirations.

In some respects, there was good advice in this, but only to a point. The writer was trying to be helpful and convince the teen to be all that he or she wanted to be. The problem came with the idea that it was all up to him or her. "Just go out and engineer yourself" was the recommendation. That kind of thinking can provide fertile soil for the growth of self-righteous prayers. It is only when we know our position before God that we can begin to pray rightly. When we know our place and express it, we will be praying in a way that God hears.

I Call for Mercy

This final characteristic of humble prayer is seen in what is asked for. The tax collector was passionate about help that only God can give. We either stand with the Pharisee, trusting in what we have accomplished, or we stand with the tax collector, whose only hope was God. When we pray, it is not to alert God to what we have managed to achieve but to admit that we desperately need Him. "The pride of the Pharisee was based on his lack of need for God. He didn't need God to help him accomplish his limited view of righteousness."[16] Only by acknowledging our need of mercy can it be found. If we are too proud to admit just how seriously we require God, His pity, and His forgiveness, then there is no reason for our prayers to be heard. That is the only basis of our entire relationship with God in the first place. "The

Gospel is not what we can do for ourselves, but what God has done for us."[17]

Prayer is a conversation that is built on that relationship, one that continues to appreciate that God alone is the source of our much-needed mercy. "God's generosity and mercy reaches out to the lost, and it can be received only by the person concerned acknowledging his need of that mercy."[18] Therefore, that recognition of our neediness before God must be expressed in prayer.

Recently I came across Dallas Willard's version of the Lord's Prayer. Even though it is more of a paraphrase than a translation, I was impressed enough to memorize it so that I could pray it regularly. I also taught it to my family so that we could pray it together.

Dear Father always near us,
may your name be treasured and loved,
may your rule be completed in us—
may your will be done here on earth
in just the way it is done in heaven.
Give us today the things we need today,
and forgive us our sins and impositions on you
as we are forgiving all who in any way offend us.
Please don't put us through trials,
but deliver us from everything bad.
Because you are the one in charge,
and you have all the power,
and the glory too is all yours—forever—
Which is just the way we want it![19]

This version of the familiar prayer helped me to see that the way Jesus taught His disciples to pray had all the elements described by the parable under discussion. Jesus' teaching was ever consistent, ever cohesive. The

Lord's Prayer begins, continues, and ends with the expressed desire that God would be in His place. This is true in that the Father is seen as the supreme and universal ruler. The prayer declares God to be the One who has all the authority and ability in the universe. Further, the prayer puts me in my place, as the one who is not in charge, calling upon the One who is. It defines my place as the one who is willing to submit to the greater will of the heavenly Father. Finally, the prayer is a cry for mercy, for it requests from God the forgiveness of my sins. It also reminds me that if I'm expecting God's mercy, I must be equally forgiving of those who antagonize me in any and every way. Understanding this has given me a new appreciation for this prayer Jesus taught His followers. My interest has been renewed in this as a model and guide for my prayer life.

The parable closed with this comment from Jesus: "I tell you that this man, rather than the other, went home justified before God. For everyone who exalts himself will be humbled, and he who humbles himself will be exalted" (Luke 18:14). *Justified.* What a powerful word. What an incredible result from a single prayer. God declared the tax collector righteous. His sin was blotted out, washed away, removed "as far as the east is from the west" (Psalm 103:12). God heard his prayer and accepted him. "Pride always leaves us unfulfilled and unsatisfied. Humility opens the floodgates of the heart of God; it's the basic ingredient of any prayer that God will answer."[20] Praying rightly is serious business.

The implication of Jesus' words was that the Pharisee went away unjustified. Because the man was more interested in exalting himself, he was brought low. It was the other man who came before the Lord in great humility that in the end was lifted up.

This is a theme throughout Scripture. "He mocks proud mockers but gives grace to the humble," Proverbs 3:34 states. After he quoted this Old Testament passage, the apostle Peter gave us these familiar words in his letter: "Humble yourselves, therefore, under God's mighty hand, that he may lift you up in due time. Cast all your anxiety on him because he cares for you" (1 Peter 5:6–7). It was no mere coincidence that Peter spoke about our need for humility and followed that with promised relief when we throw our worries onto God. It is only when we are able to humble ourselves before the Maker of the Universe that we can begin to rightly unburden ourselves in prayer and trust Him to untangle our messes and empower us to live through our troubles. Such humility is so important because God opposes the proud but gives grace to and pronounces justified all the humble ones.

Howard Hendricks told the story of a man who heard the good news about Jesus one Thursday evening and came to church on Sunday as a brand-new follower of Christ.

> The pastor announced that we were going to have an evening service, and of course the guy didn't know enough to stay home. So he showed up again. That's when he learned that our church had a Bible study and prayer meeting on Wednesday night, so he came that evening as well.
>
> I sat next to him at the prayer meeting, and just before we got started, he turned to me and asked, "Do you think they'd mind if I prayed?"
>
> "Of course not," I reassured him. "That's what we're here for."
>
> "Yeah, I know," he said, "but I've got a problem. I can't pray the way you people do."

I told him, "That's no problem, friend. You should thank God for that!"

Well, we started praying, and I could tell he was too nervous to take part. Finally, I put my hand on his thigh to encourage him. I'll never forget his prayer: "Lord, this is Jim," he began. "I'm the one who met you last Thursday night. I'm sorry, Lord, because I can't say it the way the rest of these people do, but I want to tell you the best I know how. I love you, Lord. I really do. Thanks a lot. I'll see you later."

I tell you, that prayer ignited our prayer meeting! Some of us had been doing a good job of talking about theology in prayer—you know, exploring the universe of doctrine, scraping the Milky Way with our big words. But this guy prayed.[21]

It is not those prayers that are full of religious veneer and self-confidence that receive God's undivided attention. Instead, it is those prayers that are humble and honest, those prayers that are truly cries for help that gain a hearing with God. It is the prayer prayed by the unassuming sinner, not the prayer of the presuming preener that gains anything with the Father in heaven. Therefore, I will pray with these five objectives in mind.

- I will direct my prayers to God alone.
- I will be honest, open, and reverently intimate with my heavenly Father.
- I will exalt Him, as I seek to be unpretentious myself.
- I will resist the temptation to use others as a gauge for my strengths or weaknesses.
- I will be more interested in His will than in my own.

It is in the humble prayer that God pronounces us justified. No crystal bowl or healing blue light required.

Notes

1. Dallas Willard, *The Divine Conspiracy* (San Francisco: Harper, 1998), 241–42.
2. Ibid., 243.
3. William Hendriksen, *Exposition of the Gospel According to Luke,* New Testament Commentary (Grand Rapids: Baker, 1984), 9:818–19.
4. Gary Inrig, *The Parables* (Grand Rapids: Discovery House, 1991), 166.
5. David Wenham, *The Parables of Jesus* (Downers Grove, Ill.: Inter-Varsity, 1989), 118.
6. Hendriksen, *Exposition of the Gospel According to Luke,* 819.
7. William Barclay, *The Daily Study Bible: The Gospel of Luke* (Philadelphia: Westminster, 1956), 233.
8. Alexander MacLaren, *Expositions of Holy Scripture,* vol. 9, *St. Luke* (reprint, Grand Rapids: Baker, 1984), 135.
9. Norval Geldenhuys, *Commentary on the Gospel of Luke,* The New International Commentary on the New Testament, ed. F. F. Bruce (1951; reprint, Grand Rapids: Discovery House, 1991), 451.
10. Lloyd John Ogilvie, *The Autobiography of God* (Glendale, Calif.: Regal, 1979), 192.
11. Douglas Beyer, *Parables for Christian Living* (Valley Forge, Pa.: Judson, 1985), 99–100.
12. Hendriksen, *Exposition of the Gospel According to Luke,* 819.
13. F. Godet, *A Commentary on the Gospel of St. Luke,* trans. M. D. Cusin (Edinburgh: T & T Clark, n.d.), 2:204.
14. H. A. Ironside, *Addresses on the Gospel of Luke* (New York: Loizeaux, 1955), 549.
15. Inrig, *The Parables,* 162.
16. Ogilvie, *Autobiography of God,* 196.
17. Beyer, *Parables for Christian Living,* 102.
18. Wenham, *The Parables of Jesus,* 120.
19. Willard, *The Divine Conspiracy,* 269.
20. Ogilvie, *Autobiography of God,* 198.
21. Howard Hendricks, *Standing Together* (Gresham, Oreg.: Vision House, 1995).

chapter ten

Using What You've Got

"The Talents"
Luke 19:11–27

During the fall of 1988, there was mild hysteria in some circles over the return of Christ. A book written by former NASA rocket engineer Edgar Wisenant fueled the frenzy. The book was entitled *88 Reasons Why the Rapture Will Be in 1988*. Some groups of people did some out-of-the-ordinary things in preparation for the Second Coming. On September 12, 1988, the *Toronto Star* reported a few of the reactions. "Some Christians are selling off their valuables in anticipation that they will soon be in the Kingdom of God. A Durham, N.C., television station reported that several residents last week put their cars and a boat up for sale in anticipation of the event."

I have never understood this kind of reaction. Why would you bother selling your possessions if you believed Christ was returning tomorrow? Might you need cash in the kingdom? Do you want to make sure that someone is enjoying your boat once you are gone? The only rational reason I can imagine is that these people didn't really think they should have bought that particular car or boat in the first place, and so were divesting themselves of it before Christ comes back.

As I write these words, millennial fever has afflicted many in our world. The dawn of a new millennium has given rise to much speculation and strange behavior. One of the cities most affected is Jerusalem. Millennial fever grips that city, as numbers of people locate there in preparation for the end of human history. One particular hotel was reported as having these guests all staying there at one time: the apostles Peter and Paul, King David, the angels Michael and Gabriel, and not one but two messiahs. Why these odd reactions? They are not a new phenomenon at all. In fact, it was just such a scenario that Jesus had to address with a parable.

Jesus had just announced the salvation of the tax collector Zacchaeus. A true transformation had taken place in this man's life. Jesus proclaimed that this was why He had come, to seek and to save the lost (Luke 19:10). With those words ringing in the ears of the people, Jesus told a parable. Notice the very specific reason He told this story at this time. "While they were listening to this, he went on to tell them a parable, because he was near Jerusalem and the people thought that the kingdom of God was going to appear at once" (Luke 19:11).

Like those who gather in Jerusalem today, these people saw Jesus' proximity to the city as the proper time for the kingdom of God to come. The crowds were expecting an immediate reign. "The word for 'appear' is a strong one. It means coming into clear, outward, open manifestation."[1] The people wanted an instant takeover, with Jesus conquering the Roman government and setting the Jewish people free from their control.

In response to this desire, Jesus communicated that

the kingdom was not going to happen right away. Rather than getting frenzied about that and reacting in some bizarre fashion, the people should get to work on gospel tasks, He told them.

> He said: "A man of noble birth went to a distant country to have himself appointed king and then to return. So he called ten of his servants and gave them ten minas. 'Put this money to work,' he said, 'until I come back.'
>
> "But his subjects hated him and sent a delegation after him to say, 'We don't want this man to be our king.'
>
> "He was made king, however, and returned home. Then he sent for the servants to whom he had given the money, in order to find out what they had gained with it." (Luke 19:12–15)

Almost without exception, commentators mention the connection between this parable and a real-life event some thirty years before. Some even call it the only parable Jesus told that was based upon an actual historical event. The historical event in question involved Archelaus and his desire for a portion of the kingdom left by Herod the Great. Archelaus had received Judea and went to Rome to petition to become the royal ruler. He was so hated for his butchery that a delegation of fifty citizens was sent to plead to Caesar that he not make Archelaus their king. Caesar confirmed Archelaus' right to govern Judea but did not allow him the title of king. After nine years of barbarous rule, Archelaus was banished to Vienna.[2]

I am unconvinced that this is what Jesus had in mind. There are certainly similarities, but the main facts of the story are quite divergent from the point Jesus made. What this historical background does provide, however, is the understanding that the parable presented a situation that was common for the day. Although somewhat unusual in our frame of reference, noblemen did have to petition far countries for the right to become king. Citizens did have the right to protest such appointments. With that in mind, take a closer look at the story.

The nobleman was on his way to a far place to be crowned king. In his absence he gave ten servants money to invest. Each of them received the same amount, a mina. This unit was equal to one hundred drachmas. A drachma buys very little today, and one hundred of them would only purchase a bottle of water in modern Athens. However, in that day a drachma was the going rate for a day of labor. So this mina was equivalent to one hundred days' wages. (Please don't confuse this story with another that Jesus told. It is recorded in Matthew 25. In that parable, the amount given to each servant was different. Here it is the same.) With his mina each servant was to do business.

Then the man who would be king departed, leaving the servants to put his money to work. There was a group of citizens that was not at all sorry to see him go, for they detested him and had no intention of allowing him to be their king. In order to prevent his ascension to the throne, a delegation was sent to protest, but the demonstration failed. The nobleman returned a king and called his servants to give account of how each one had handled his money.

Through the story, Jesus was certainly talking about Himself, and among other lessons, He referred to the timing of His kingdom. "Obviously this parable teaches that Jesus predicted an interval of time between his ascension and return."[3] But the main point concerned what Christ's servants should do until He comes back. What are we doing with what He gave us?

The way that we understand the parable is linked to what the mina stands for. Remember that in contrast to the parable of the talents, each servant got the same amount. So we can't understand the mina to be spiritual gifts, material possessions, or human talents. Many commentators identify the identical amounts of money as representing the gospel. "The grace of salvation common to all believers."[4] "Now, what is the thing in which all Christians are alike? . . . the message of salvation which we call the Gospel of the blessed Lord."[5] "That which we all have in equal measure: the gospel of Jesus Christ."[6]

Every one of us who believes on Jesus Christ, who has become a child of God through faith in Jesus, belongs to Him. We are people who are entrusted with the good news about Jesus, people who bear His name and are His representatives on this earth. The question in this parable is, What have we done with that responsibility? As we wait for the King to return, what are we doing with what we have been given? The main point of the parable can be expressed in this sentence: *Our business with Christ now determines our destiny.* Jesus presented three categories of people that He would find upon His return and what each group will receive.

FOR THE FAITHFUL, THERE WILL BE REWARD

I graduated from college in May of 1980. Although I had no clear idea of what was ahead, I had no concerns either. I moved back home with Mom and Dad, bought a car, and was confident that God would take over from there. Looking back now, that was probably quite a scary time for my parents. They must have been very interested as I contemplated going on to seminary and weighed that against getting right into ministry. Not long after my return home, our church custodian had a heart attack. Someone approached me about filling in until he recovered. I didn't even think twice about it. The ink was barely dry on my bachelor of science degree, and suddenly I was a custodian.

Frankly, I tackled that job as if it was the one I had been training for my entire life. I did it as well as I possibly could, which amazed my mother, given the disastrous condition of my room during that time. Since it was hourly work, and I moved at a rate ten times faster than had my dear predecessor, I did the job in much less time. The building was clean, the church saved money, and I was a part-time janitor.

Even when I did additional things that weren't on the list, my hours barely reached a twenty a week. That included the day I waxed the piano and the minister of music told me never, ever to do that again. I made several such mistakes, but they were all in the vein of doing the best job I could do.

As I vacuumed halls, buffed floors, and scrubbed toilets, an opportunity for full-time ministry appeared at another church. I was in no hurry to consider it, although I still have the letter my dad wrote for me expressing my interest in the position. Then at the end of the summer, my home church, where currently I was custodian, asked if I would consider becoming the full-time youth pastor. The janitor was recovering nicely and seemed ready to return to his duties. I accepted the call and began my ministry.

I have always felt that the reason the church considered me at that time had at least a little to do with my willingness to be the custodian and the faithfulness with which I did the job. It also may have been due to the fact that the custodian wasn't well, and that I could be handy at a moment's notice. But I seriously feel that because I had proven myself in the smaller things, the church was willing to entrust me with larger issues.

In God's economy, faithfulness is rewarded. That is certainly a significant point in this parable of Jesus. Of the ten servants to whom the king gave a mina, there were a couple who responded faithfully, and those two were richly rewarded.

> "The first one came and said, 'Sir, your mina has earned ten more.'
>
> "'Well done, my good servant!' his master replied. 'Because you have been trustworthy in a very small matter, take charge of ten cities.'
>
> "The second came and said, 'Sir, your mina has earned five more.'
>
> "His master answered, 'You take charge of five cities.'" (Luke 19:16–19)

Notice the humility in evidence here. Both of these servants had greatly increased their allotment, but both of them still referred to it as "your mina." Why did they work and invest even though in the end it would all belong to the king anyway? Because they were faithful. Since they could be trusted with this small thing, the king gave them great responsibility.

They were not the possessors, the owners, of the cities, but each servant administered, ruled over them for the king. The size of that reward was linked to their faithfulness. "A great responsibility rests on each one of His followers to work faithfully until He comes."[7] For those of us who have been made children of God through faith in Christ and given a new name and every spiritual blessing in Christ, we are to do His business faithfully until He returns. This activity does not get us into heaven.

That is only decided by what we do with Jesus. But our faithful activity does determine our reward.

Our concepts of heaven are frequently so flawed. They have been infected with Hollywood inventions and anemic comic descriptions. Many of us envision heaven as some type of eternal worship service. There we sit, bored and barely awake, wondering *How long will he preach today?* Our minds see snippets of clouds, innocuous music, and angel's wings. Our grand vision of a glorious eternity has devolved into hymns, harps, and hard pews forever. Certainly that is nothing to be excited about, nor to look forward to.

That is not the picture of heaven that is presented to us in Scripture. Heaven is the place Christ is preparing for us right now. In the glorious dwelling He has made, we will enjoy things in ways of which we can now only dream. In his classic work from the 1600s, *The Saints Everlasting Rest,* Richard Baxter spoke of that scene. "This rest contains a sweet and constant action of all the powers of the soul and body in this enjoyment of God. It is not the rest of a stone."[8]

No, this is an active, productive rest. A rest which is filled to the full with all knowledge, love, wisdom, delight, and peace. As Baxter put it, "We shall derive its joys immediately from God."[9] From this parable and other teachings of Jesus, we catch a glimpse of what those joys will be. The picture that emerges shows an eternity that is dynamic, creative, busy, and filled with responsibility.

"We will see him in the stunning surroundings that he had with the Father before the beginning of the created cosmos. And we will actively participate in the future governance of the universe. We will not sit around looking at one another or at God for eternity but will join the eternal Logos, 'reign with him,' in the endlessly ongoing creative work of God."[10] Heaven is not passive adoration but passionate responsibility. "A life of joy and service in God's presence."[11] We will be empowered to join in the cosmic creativity of God's universe.

Just as these two servants received cities over which to rule for their king, so we will receive ruling responsibilities from the King of Kings. We will participate in the administration of His universe. "Similarly, the Lord Jesus Christ, at his glorious return will praise his faithful servants and will reward them in proportion to the degree of faithfulness they have shown. They will be given an opportunity to render even greater service in the new and heaven and earth."[12]

That reward we enjoy—the responsibility we receive —is based upon our faithfulness now. As Paul writes to believers in 2 Corinthians 5:10, "For we must all appear before the judgment seat of Christ, that each one may receive what is due him for the things done while in the body, whether good or bad." We will give an accounting for the valuable and the worthless things that we have done. Since this is so, the Lord of glory deserves our best, even in smallest of things. We must be encouraged to keep on, to remain faithful, because when He comes we will be greatly rewarded.

There are many reading these pages who have done far more for the kingdom than I will ever dream of doing. Stay faithful. Radiate the light of Christ wherever you go. You are bearers of the glorious good news about Jesus. Let it shine. Faithfully live, serve, teach, help, counsel, give, love, mend, forgive, testify, and minister; and when the King of Kings returns He will say, "Well done, my good servant. Because you've been faithful here, you will be richly rewarded." The rewarding of the

faithful is the first category of people Christ will find at
His return. Notice the second category of people, who
are represented by the third servant.

FOR THE NEGLIGENT,
THERE WILL BE LOSS

There is an old joke about heaven that has been kicking around for years. Like most jokes about eternity, it
gives a thoroughly inaccurate picture of the life to come.
After living a wild life, given to wine, women, and song,
Ned finally died. Since he had spent most of his earthly
existence pursuing all the pleasures he could find, Ned
was shocked when he stood before the pearly gates.

At the gates he met Saint Peter. "There must be some
mistake," Ned said. "I never expected to get in here."

"There's no mistake," Peter replied. "You see, we
don't keep records."

Amazed and relieved, Ned followed Peter inside the
heavenly gates. As they walked through the city, the pair
came upon a group of people who were crying, wailing
their regrets, and screaming with great remorse. Every
so often, they would kick one another in the posterior.
"What's wrong with those guys?" Ned asked.

Peter said, "They thought we kept records too."

The truth is, records *are* kept. We will give an account of what we have done or not done. There is a cor-
relation between our lives in the King's absence and
what will happen when He returns.

> "Then another servant came and said, 'Sir, here is your
> mina; I have kept it laid away in a piece of cloth. I was
> afraid of you, because you are a hard man. You take out
> what you did not put in and reap what you did not sow.'
>
> "His master replied, 'I will judge you by your own
> words, you wicked servant! You knew, did you, that I am a

hard man, taking out what I did not put in, and reaping what I did not sow? Why then didn't you put my money on deposit, so that when I came back, I could have collected it with interest?'

"Then he said to those standing by, 'Take his mina away from him and give it to the one who has ten minas.'

"'Sir,'" they said, "'he already has ten!'"

"He replied, 'I tell you that to everyone who has, more will be given, but as for the one who has nothing, even what he has will be taken away.'" (Luke 19:20–26)

This servant had simply held on to the coin. He also referred to the money as "your mina," but there was no hint of humility in this; it was an accusation. In effect the servant said, "I squirreled it away so you could have your precious coin back. You should be thankful that I was so cautious."

It is interesting that the cloth in which the servant preserved the mina was one used as a sweat rag, or to blow one's nose, or to wrap the head of a corpse. The servant could not be commended for his careful conservation. Surely it would have been risky to invest, to put the money to work, but that was what he was told to do. By safeguarding the mina, he had disobeyed his master.

This servant was full of attitude. He accused the king of being harsh, unfair, rough, and rigid. The king said, "Liar! If you really believed that you would have tried harder. If you were so afraid of me, then you would have done something rather than nothing." The king suggested that his servant could have at least put mina on the moneylender's bench in order to gain a little interest. "Since moneylenders paid interest on money deposited with them, which in turn they would lend out at a higher rate of interest, it follows that our modern banking system had its origin here, the very word *bank* being derived from this word *bench*."[13] This servant attempted nothing, risked nothing, and gained nothing. As a result, he had the mina taken away.

This servant represents those followers of Christ who are negligent in following the Master's instructions. They do little or nothing with the glorious gift entrusted to them. "Although no believer can perish, the unfaithful and those who forsake their vocation will meet with disgrace and loss."[14]

It may strike against our sense of fairness that the servant would lose what he was given. It may seem quite unjust that the mina was given to the servant who already had the most. This reflected God's economy. The faithful received even more, and the negligent lost what little he had. "Whosoever neglects his opportunities and is unfaithful in the Lord's service will become spiritually impoverished, will receive still fewer opportunities for service and will appear poor and naked before His throne at [H]is second advent."[15]

It is possible to be a Christian, a true child of God, to gain heaven, but have nothing else to show for it. This is the point that the apostle Paul made when he spoke of the building materials we use in life and what will happen to them in eternity. Only one foundation will remain, and that foundation is Jesus. The quality of our works built on that foundation will face God's test by fire. "If what he has built survives, he will receive his reward. If it is burned up, he will suffer loss; he himself will be saved, but only as one escaping through the flames" (1 Corinthians 3:14–15).

That is why we are told to continue in Christ, so that we can be confident and unashamed when He comes. You say you belong to Christ? Don't take it for granted, and don't disguise yourself so that no one ever knows. Don't neglect to invest what God has given you for His glory now, or one day you will suffer loss. Not eternal loss, but the loss of reward. "Throw your Christianity on the trash heap, or else let God be the *Lord* of your life . . . but don't wrap him up in your handkerchief."[16]

I have learned not to judge Christians who appear to be doing nothing, because often they are serving in ways I know nothing about. But I have known a few who appeared so inactive for Christ, people who showed so few vital signs that a funeral seemed to be in order. One woman taught school for twenty-five years, and no one around her had the slightest idea she was a Christian. She had professed Christ and joined the church decades before, but there had been no sign of life since. She did her job; she traveled and enjoyed life in many ways. She was somewhat involved in community events, but Christ was shrouded in a hanky, carefully preserved, pickled. That type of life seems fine to many now, but when the King comes back, such people will be naked and embarrassed. The negligent are a group of people who will suffer loss when Christ returns. Now the focus of the parable turns to a third category of people.

FOR THE REJECTERS,
THERE WILL BE JUDGMENT

It's a Wonderful Life is a good movie. Although the film was not originally very successful, it has gone on to take its place among the favorite films in modern America. I know that some people complain about the ending. Of course, the ending is happy enough. George Bailey (Jimmy Stewart) realizes he does have a wonderful life. He has everything that matters, including friends, and he is doing something that matters. The problem people have is that justice isn't served in the film. George escapes the penalty and scandal of embezzlement, but old man Potter gets off free. This vile old man does not receive what he deserves at the end, at least that we can see. We can only assume that he died a warped, frustrated old man. But in the short term, he has the "embezzled" money in his gnarled fist, and no one is the wiser.

We like stories with happy endings, but some endings require justice in order to be truly complete. With that in mind, we can see this parable as complete. "We might wish that Jesus had concluded his teaching ministry with some upbeat stories with 'happily-ever-after endings,' but he didn't. The last two stories he told end with executions."[17]

That was exactly how this story ended, with a sentence of capital punishment being carried out on the king's enemies. "But those enemies of mine who did not want me to be king over them—bring them here and kill them in front of me" (Luke 19:27). This was a third group, quite different from the others. These were not the faithful, whom he rewarded. They were not the negligent, who lost all reward. These were the master's adversaries, those who rejected him as king. Their attitude was clear from the beginning. "We don't want you. Anyone but you." So the king had them executed right in front of him.

This sounds brutally cruel, especially if you have only seen God as a harmless, happy old man who wouldn't keep anyone out of His heaven in the end. But do not fail to notice that this king was only hard on those who were negligent, disobedient, or openly rebellious. The facts are plain. "A fatal end awaits everyone who refuses to acknowledge and to obey Jesus as King and Lord."[18] All those who refuse the rule of Christ, who insist on doing it "my way," who fail to bend the knee in submission will suffer eternally.

Jesus said that at the end of the age He will send His angels to weed out all evildoers, who will then be thrown "into the fiery furnace, where there will be weeping and gnashing of teeth" (Matthew 13:50). This is the stark reality. For all those who refuse the reign of Jesus Christ, those who reject His right to rule over them, there is the most severe judgment. Justice is served, and it is a scary thing.

Just as these citizens attempted to stop this nobleman from becoming their king, so did Jesus' own people reject Him. All attempts to derail the reign of Christ have failed and will ultimately fail. All opposition movements will be frustrated. His kingdom will supplant all others. "The stone the builders rejected has become the capstone; the LORD has done this, and it is marvelous in our eyes" (Psalm 118:22–23). These words are applied to Jesus. Despite the seeming victory of His enemies in putting Jesus on the cross, the Rejected One triumphed. The day of final victory is coming—the time when all accounts will be settled. Those who opposed, rejected, ignored, and rebelled will be judged. The voices of heaven will announce the glorious and final reality: "The kingdom of the world has become the kingdom of our Lord and of his Christ, and he will reign for ever and ever" (Revelation 11:15).

* * *

The great lady was dying. Mrs. Theophilus was wealthy, but there was no denying death. The doctor was certain she would not last the night. She called her household together—the cook, the maid, the chauffeur, and the gardener. Since her only child had died years before, this was all the family Theophilus had. All four had been with her for years. There were tears as they gathered around the frail form. She spoke so softly that they had to lean toward her just to hear her final words.

The words were of her concern for them and their future. She informed them that the bulk of her estate would go to set up the property as a home for unwed expectant mothers. The four employees would be able to keep their jobs as long as they wanted. But this was not all; she did have something of value for each of them. There was breathless anticipation as the elderly woman weakly gestured at a box on her nightstand. The box contained four jewelry cases. Inside the cases were identical necklaces. Each necklace was made of a heavy gold chain adorned with a bejeweled pendant. The pendant had a rather peculiar design. She encouraged each of them to put the necklace on. As they stood before her, the gold weighed heavily on their necks and glittered in the low light.

"I want you to wear these as much as you can. I want you to remember me in this way." She paused for a moment, taking a slow breath. Just when they wondered if she was gone, the great lady spoke again.

"Adorn yourselves with this expensive piece, that others will see beyond what you are, to who you are. With this necklace you will not be merely a cook, maid, gardener, or chauffeur; you will be my sons and daughters, carrying on the Theophilus name." With that she dismissed them amid tears, kisses, and good-byes.

The cook didn't wait for the funeral. He saw the necklace as ghastly, and he had no intention of ever wearing it. When the jeweler told him the value, he sold it without batting an eye. He quit his job the next day, never having enjoyed cooking for the old bat in the first place. There was a time he had considered poisoning her once or twice anyway and so he was glad she was dead. He certainly had no intention of whipping up gourmet meals for a bunch of undiscerning promiscuous women and their illegitimate children.

The gardener quickly made her way to a jeweler as well. Seeing what the cook had done, she guessed that the necklace might be valuable. Still, she was shocked to learn just how much it was worth. It made her very uncomfortable to have it on. She spent an entire night awake, terrified that she might lose it or that it would be stolen. The truth was she considered the piece to be rather unattractive anyway. So the day after the funeral she rented a safe-deposit box and locked the necklace away for the future. She stayed on as a gardener because it was a secure job, but her new early retirement plan was to eventually sell the necklace and never touch dirt again.

The maid and the chauffeur were different. Both constantly wore their gifts, just as Mrs. Theophilus had requested. Both dearly loved their mistress and would have stayed had she left them nothing. They adjusted to the changes in their jobs. The maid cared for a constantly changing number of pregnant women and their new babies. The chauffeur drove them to and from the hospital at all hours of the day and night.

One year after the great lady's death, her lawyer arrived. He summoned the staff before him. There were now only three, the cook having become an investment banker. The lawyer announced that there was a codicil to the will. As he read the codicil, there were gasps of astonishment. The will demanded that on this anniversary date of Theophilus's death, any employee wearing the necklace would become the administrator, the agent of the estate.

The lawyer noticed that the maid was wearing her necklace at that very moment. The chauffeur panicked as he touched his neck and felt nothing. Suddenly he remembered that he had taken the necklace off as he polished the limousine earlier that day. The heavy piece of jewelry was in his coat pocket, and he swiftly placed it back on. The gardener was frantic. "If you will just wait I can be back in an hour with mine," she begged. Then, realizing that it was Saturday afternoon and the bank was closed until Monday, she pleaded for a longer reprieve.

"I will wait until Monday," the attorney replied. "Then when you bring it to me, I will take it and have it sold and the money divided between these two." The gardener wailed, she shrieked, she yelled, all to no avail. She worked the rest of her days in Theophilus's house.

The former cook lost his fortune in the great crash of January 1, 2000, and died a penniless drunk.

The maid and the chauffeur were immediately given important places of responsibility, with commensurate salaries, expansive offices, lavish living quarters, a large staff, and the legal name of Theophilus, which, by the way, means lover of God.

* * *

The King of Kings has left us with a glorious treasure, the gospel of Christ. The question is what will we do with it until He comes back? What is my attitude toward the glorious gift of the good news? Am I living as a conservationist, an undercover double agent, a maintenance man, a survivalist who is barely hanging on until my King returns? As a loyal servant of God, here is how I should respond to Jesus' words in this parable.

- I should be willing to risk it all in obedient faith.
- I should long to have something to offer my Master when He returns.
- I should not doubt that the Lord of the universe will settle all accounts one day.
- I should produce for Christ in joyful expectation of the reward and responsibility that He will assign to all His faithful ones.

Our business with Christ *now* determines our destiny. There will be judgment for those who reject Him, loss for the negligent, and great reward for those who are faithful. Make His business your own. Take risks that He will reward. Use what you've been given. Put on the Lord Jesus. Wear Him well. Keep on in faithfulness until He comes, and you will not be disappointed.

Notes

1. G. Campbell Morgan, *The Parables and Metaphors of Our Lord* (New York: Revell, 1943), 244.
2. Flavius Josephus, *The Life and Words of Flavius Josephus,* trans. William Whiston (Philadelphia: Universal Book & Bible, n.d.), 516–672.
3. Walter Liefeld, in *The Expositor's Bible Commentary,* ed. Frank E. Gaebelein, D. A. Carson, Walter W. Wessel, and Walter L. Liefield (Grand Rapids: Zondervan, 1984), 8:1009.
4. F. Godet, *A Commentary on the Gospel of St. Luke,* trans. M. D. Cusin (Edinburgh: T & T Clark, n.d.), 2:221.
5. Alexander MacLaren, *Expositions of Scripture,* vol. 9, *St. Luke* (reprint, Grand Rapids: Baker, 1984), 165.
6. Douglas Beyer, *Parables for Christian Living* (Valley Forge, Pa.: Judson, 1985), 108.
7. Norval Geldenhuys, *Commentary on the Gospel of Luke,* The New International Commentary on the New Testament, ed. F. F. Bruce, (Grand Rapids: Eerdmans, 1979), 474.

8. Richard Baxter, *The Saints Everlasting Rest,* abridg. Benjamin Fawcett (New York: American Tract, 1884), 32.

9. Ibid., 65.

10. Dallas Willard, *The Divine Conspiracy* (San Francisco: Harper, 1998), 378.

11. David Wenham, *The Parables of Jesus* (Downers Grove, Ill.: Inter-Varsity, 1989), 88.

12. William Hendriksen, *Exposition of the Gospel According to Luke,* New Testament Commentary (Grand Rapids: Baker, 1984), 9:861.

13. Ibid., 862.

14. Geldenhuys, *Commentary on the Gospel of Luke,* 475.

15. Ibid.

16. Helmut Thielicke, *The Waiting Father,* trans. John Doberstein, (New York: Harper & Row, 1959), 145.

17. Beyer, *Parables for Christian Living,* 106.

18. Geldenhuys, *Commentary on the Gospel of Luke,* 475.

REVIEW AND STUDY GUIDE

James S. Bell Jr.

Chapter One

1. We have various hearing "impairments" in terms of hearing God's Word that may limit our productiveness on His behalf.

2. One of the main reasons we have not prepared our hearts to receive God's Word is that we are overwhelmed by our circumstances, trying to cope with them on our own.

3. Strong emotions are often included in a positive response to God's Word but are not a sufficient foundation in themselves to bear enduring fruit.

4. We need to clean up our character, or have a noble heart, before we can truly receive God's Word and allow it to penetrate our hearts.

5. When we do take possession of the truth, we need to hang on to it through life's trials, allowing it even in hard times to encourage and instruct us.

QUESTIONS AND RESPONSE

1. In what ways are you hearing impaired—allowing distractions, rebellion, or other issues to keep you partially deaf to God's commands?

2. When in your life have you thought you had true commitment to God's Word to change you, when it was actually mainly emotion? What was the missing ingredient necessary for change?

Chapter Two

POINTS TO CONSIDER

1. The two greatest commandments show us clearly how unable we are to meet God's standards of love, yet Jesus Himself did it for us.

2. Sometimes when we see people in serious trouble, we actually thank God we don't share their difficulties, rather than enduring their inconvenience or danger and meeting their need.

3. As with Jews and Samaritans, we need to leap racial, ethnic, and religious barriers to help those who are hurting, sometimes partially due to their minority status.

4. We cannot just feel sorry for or speak out on behalf of the Samaritans in our lives; we must act out of our personal resources.

5. At times it can be difficult to recognize God's divine appointments in chance meetings or unplanned encounters with those who are hurting, but we need to be under the guidance of the Holy Spirit and through Him be alert to such opportunities.

QUESTIONS AND RESPONSE

1. Be honest with yourself and admit the times you acted like the priest and Levite when faced with someone in great need. Allow God to deal with those areas in your heart.

2. To be fair to yourself, recall the times where you sacrificed yourself for someone else, perhaps at great expense. What did you do right that could be repeated at the next opportunity?

Chapter Three

1. We should never hesitate, but persevere in prayer, because we always need God for the most basic needs all the way to the most extraordinary ones.

2. Boldness means that we can ask God anytime without reserve for the things that we need, having no fear or shame in seeking what we want, instead of being passive or laid back.

3. Just as earthly fathers have wisdom in what to give their children, our heavenly Father knows how and what to give us in response to our prayers.

4. The Holy Spirit is the greatest gift we can receive from our Father when asking for things, for He provides everything we need to live a life of victory and blessing.

5. At times our requests are small because we're afraid to be audacious and bold with God; yet if we simply ask God, He can do great things.

QUESTIONS AND RESPONSE

1. What are your main reasons for not asking for big things from God or for not asking persistently? Ask yourself how this might limit your understanding of God's nature.

2. Think back on an occasion when God's answer to your prayer surprised you. What did the answer say about God's wisdom in giving in His own way?

Chapter Four

1. When our main focus is on acquiring more and more material possessions, we are guilty of greed, and the result is spiritual poverty.

2. Though God is not opposed to our enjoyment of life, our retirement goals, spending patterns, and generosity levels should not be geared to self-indulgence.

3. When we experience success we often forget that God is the originator and owner of that success and has a right to determine what we do with it—He can withdraw it at any time.

4. A life in pursuit of money and power is an empty, sad life with no true security; without it all, we would be more inclined to trust God.

5. Sometimes our wisest investments in a high quality of life mean stepping away from luxuries, career advancement, and other pleasures in order to please God and others.

QUESTIONS AND RESPONSE

1. When have questions like "dividing the inheritance" taken precedence over larger spiritual commitments? Why was your mind divided?

2. Which do you think of more—your bank balance or your spiritual riches—and how can you refocus more on the latter?

Chapter Five

POINTS TO CONSIDER

1. Jesus allowed no other attachments in life to take precedence over wholehearted devotion to Him. He did not attract others by meeting their "felt needs."

2. Following Christ demands all that we have, all the time; and if we aren't prepared for this commitment, we won't be able to complete our discipleship.

3. Impulsive commitments based upon emotion usually don't last, especially when we are called to discard those things that get in the way of the path God has set for us.

4. If we don't risk everything, if we hold back something in reserve, we cannot be His disciples; even though the odds are against us, God is on our side.

5. Though we need to carefully plan and count the cost ahead of time, if we aren't willing to risk everything, we may become ineffective or even useless for God.

QUESTIONS AND RESPONSE

1. When were you involved in an "earthly" task you could not finish? Why and how did you fail to plan and what did you learn?

2. What about in the spiritual realm? Have you ever made a commitment or promise to God that you failed to keep? What didn't you count on?

Chapter Six

1. God doesn't want to punish those who have turned away from Him when they return, but instead rejoices that a sinner has repented and can now be blessed as His child.

2. The older son in the parable was just as lost as the prodigal because he did not understand the nature of acceptance and forgiveness; in addition, he was blinded by his pride and self-sufficiency.

3. In the same way, we need to be careful not to judge the prodigals in our lives, realizing that we are not better and trusting in God's patience and grace to bring them home.

4. The good news is that if you are far away from God in any area of your behavior, He loves you completely and His arms are open to your return, without any condemnation.

5. We should be continually praying for the prodigals in our lives, no matter how far from God they seem to be, and we should continue to hope for those prodigals whose awful deeds do not seem to deserve God's mercy.

QUESTIONS AND RESPONSE

1. Most of us have a number of prodigals in our lives. Make a list of them and determine both to pray for them and to reach out to them in love.

2. Seek the Lord in prayer concerning the ways in which you might be a prodigal in specific areas of your own life. Ask God to give you the grace to return to Him and rejoice in your newfound freedom.

Chapter Seven

POINTS TO CONSIDER

1. The master in this parable is not commending the dishonesty of the manager, but rather his shrewdness in dealing with his difficult situation.

2. Businesspeople often use planning, discernment, and innovation for temporal gain in a way that is superior to the way Christians use worldly wealth for eternal rewards.

3. Though we cannot know immediate results when we give to missionaries or our church, we will find persons in eternity glad to receive us because of how we blessed them with our giving.

4. When we give to the causes of the kingdom of God, we are investing in our own eternal reward, but what is most amazing is that we are investing what isn't even ours, but God's.

5. Both God and money are so all-consuming that we cannot serve them both, and we will actually come to resent and hate the demands of one or the other if we try.

QUESTIONS AND RESPONSE

1. At times we say everything we have belongs to God. In reality, should being a steward rather than an owner affect how you think, plan, save, or spend? How?

2. After you have answered the seven questions found in this chapter, give yourself a rating of where you are as compared to where you want to be. Write down how you might improve in each area to achieve your goal.

Chapter Eight

1. Our eternal condition may be far different from our earthly one; we need to listen to God while on earth or accept the irreversible consequences.

2. Perhaps the greatest agony of hell is not merely suffering the absence of God but being forced to view the glory of God and yet have no part in it.

3. What we truly worship and put first is reflected in our priorities, for worship is not simply a matter of believing but of doing and will be plain for all to see.

4. We have enough revelation in the Scriptures to effectively persuade us of eternal destinies without the need for supernatural visitations or signs.

5. It is difficult to predict how people will respond to God's Word and His invitation to salvation in Christ, but it will eventually be evident in the fruit of their lives.

QUESTIONS AND RESPONSE

1. Who are the people representing Lazarus in your life—those who have physical or economic needs? What about the rich man? Are there those who are materially well off whom you can reach with the gospel before it is too late?

2. Have you, like the rich man, neglected at some point to hear the message from God and paid earthly consequences? In what ways can you better listen to God and obey His commands?

Chapter Nine

1. God does not accept prayers that focus on our own goodness or our trust in religious formulas over and above the inner needs of the soul for repentance and healing.

2. It is shocking to realize that God would hear the prayer of an habitual sinner rather than a "professional" religious person confident in his own righteousness, who shows external compliance to God's rules.

3. As we pray, comparing ourselves to others or measuring the goodness of our own actions has no validity, for only God knows our true state, and He doesn't measure it in relation to others.

4. We can truly be ourselves with God, honestly giving Him our complaints and questions, but realizing that He determines the outcome and does not owe us anything.

5. God's mercy and forgiveness are available but only as we express our needs to Him, for prayer is largely an acknowledgment of our dependence upon Him.

Questions and Response

1. Take an honest look at your overall prayer life. How much of it has elements of reminding God of the good things you've done, or subconsciously comparing yourself with others? How can you focus more on repentance and your need for Him?

2. Do you think our American Christian culture tends to lean more toward spiritual boasting and comparison, or self-denial and humility? Give reasons for your answer.

Chapter Ten

Points to Consider

1. The nature and size of our reward and future responsibilities in heaven depend upon our faithfulness to God in terms of what we have been given here.

2. In terms of God's judgment, those who are faithful will receive even more, the saved people who are negligent will suffer loss, and the enemies of God will be eternally punished.

3. Those who oppose God often appear to be victorious, but every attempt to subvert the reign of Christ will ultimately fail, up to the final day of His glorious return.

4. Our greatest treasure to utilize is not material things or even our own talents but the message of the good news of salvation in Jesus Christ.

5. In order to use effectively what God has given to us, we need to take risks by stepping out in faith and trusting that God will support our efforts that are in line with His will.

Questions and Response

1. How would you define faithfulness in the areas in which God calls you to serve? In what ways can you multiply what He has given you?

2. In what areas are you afraid to take risks to further the kingdom of God? How can you better focus on the potential eternal gain instead of the temporal loss?

Guidelines for Living Series

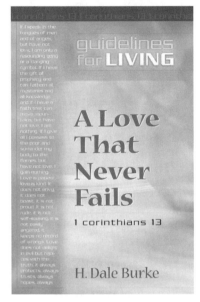

A Love That Never Fails
1 Corinthians 13
H. Dale Burke

With the world's distorted view of love, it's no wonder some Christians can't recognize godly love when they see it. God's love letter to us is 1 Corinthians 13, and it contains some of the most inspiring and practical teaching on love that the world has ever known.

Quality Paperback 0-8024-8198-1

1-800-678-8812 www.MoodyPress.org

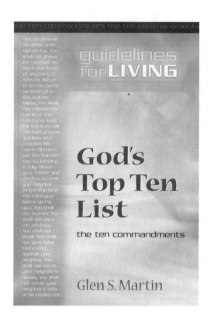

God's Top Ten List
The Ten Commandments
Glen S. Martin

Don't lie. Don't steal. The Ten Commandments might seem like just a long list of no-no's. But this in-depth book goes way beyond describing what God said and explains why He said it. He gave us this instruction list to produce happy and healthy relationships.

Quality Paperback 0-8024-3097-X

MOODY
The Name You Can Trust
1-800-678-8812 www.MoodyPress.org